Children with Special Needs in Early Childhood Settings

Identification • Intervention • Inclusion

Join us on the Web at

EarlyChildEd.delmar.com

Children with Special Needs in Early Childhood Settings

Identification • Intervention • Inclusion

CAROL L. PAASCHE • LOLA GORRILL • BEV STROM

THOMSON

DELMAR LEARNING

Australia Canada Mexico Singapore Spain United Kingdom United States

THOMSON

DELMAR LEARNING

Children with Special Needs in Early Childhood Settings
Carol L. Paasche, Lola Gorrill, Bev Strom

**Vice President,
Career Education SBU:**
Dawn Gerrain

Director of Editorial:
Sherry Gomoll

Acquisitions Editor:
Erin O'Connor

Editorial Assistant:
Ivy Ip

Director of Production:
Wendy A. Troeger

Production Editor:
Joy Kocsis

Director of Marketing:
Donna J. Lewis

Channel Manager:
Nigar Hale

Cover Design:
Dutton & Sherman

Composition:
Larry O'Brien

Printed in Canada
3 4 5 XXX 07 06 05 04

For more information contact Delmar Learning,
Executive Woods, 5 Maxwell Drive, Clifton Park, NY 12065-2919.

Or find us on the World Wide Web at www.thomsonlearning.com,
www.delmarlearning.com, or www.earlychilded.delmar.com

This book was previously published by: Pearson Education, Inc., publishing as
Addison Wesley Publishing Company.

For permission to use material from this text or product, contact us by
Tel   (800) 730-2214
Fax   (800) 730-2215
www.thomsonrights.com

Library of Congress Cataloging-in-Publication Data

Paasche, Carol L.
  Children with special needs in early childhood settings / Carol L. Paasche,
Lola Gorrill, Bev Strom.
    p. cm.
  Includes index.
  ISBN 1-4018-3570-8
    1. Children with disabilities—Education (Early childhood)—Handbooks,
manuals, etc. 2. Children—Diseases—Handbooks, manuals, etc. 3. Pediatrics—
Handbooks, manuals, etc. 4. Special education—Handbooks, manuals, etc.
I. Gorrill, Lola. II. Strom, Bev. III. Title.

LC4019.3.P33 2004
371.9'047—dc21   2003014441

NOTICE TO THE READER

TABLE OF CONTENTS

PREFACE

WHO THIS BOOK IS WRITTEN FOR

This book has been written for Early Childhood Educators and teachers who are working in settings with young children: elementary schools, preschool centers, Head Start and Early Head Start programs, child care centers, parent-child groups, and so on. The content of the text is specifically focused on children from birth to eight years of age.

We are not attempting to diagnose specific problems, but we are trying to aid teachers of young children in finding some information and programming ideas that will support them until an official assessment and diagnosis of an individual child can take place.

PURPOSE OF THIS BOOK

The main purpose of this book is four-fold.

1. To help teachers and child care personnel to recognize children whose physical, emotional, social, speech and language, overall communication skills, and/or cognitive development is different from that of other children of their age

2. To support those working with young children in knowing what questions to ask and what symptoms to look for, if they suspect there are previously unidentified concerns with regard to a child's developmental patterns

3. To know what steps to take if they have concerns about the development of a child whose condition has not been previously observed

4. To provide teachers of young children with interim interaction and program suggestions on how to work most effectively with a child presenting with a possible physical, social, emotional, behavioral, speech and language, and/or intellectual problem until outside specialists are available to offer support in programming for the specific needs of an individual child.

This book is intended as a reference guide only, *not* as a medical manual. If it is suspected that a child in your center appears to have a medical problem, discuss your observations with the parents and recommend a medical checkup. Any medical recommendations prescribed by the doctor for the child, should be followed by the center.

We are not advocating that teachers become diagnosticians or therapists; however, it must be realized that it is the teacher of young children who is often the first to recognize that a problem may exist. Observing and sharing the staff's observations and insights with the parents and the child's physician should play an important role in the child's program.

HIGHLIGHTS OF THIS BOOK

This book differs from other available resources concerned with children with special needs, in the following ways:

- The material is presented in a concise, easy-to-read, column format.

- The book is designed as a hands-on resource for those working in frontline positions with young children.

- Clear descriptions and examples, as well as up-to-date terminology, have been consistently used.

- In most listings, the middle column is used to alert teachers to other disabilities or conditions that might have similar clusters of symptoms/behaviors. Those conditions included in the text are highlighted to alert the reader that more, possibly relevant information, can be found in other sections. (**Note:** Check the Table of Contents, as some areas are subheadings of related conditions.)

- Where appropriate, we have included **Essential Information** and **Important Questions to Ask.**

- Specific **Recommendations** for working with children and families have been included in the third column. **Note:** Whereas columns 1 and 2 line up with each other, this has not been attempted in column 3, which is designed to give information relevant to all aspects of the specific special need that is the focus of the given section.

- A resource listing of relevant U.S. and Canadian organizations and Web sites has been provided at the end of each section to support early childhood teachers in obtaining additional information.

- Space has been provided for writing in additional resources applicable to the needs of an individual center or program.

- We have not included any information on laws and/or legislation relating to special needs. In researching this area, we found that there is too much variance between countries, states, and local areas, and too much detail in the legislation for meaningful inclusion in this type of text. Furthermore, there are many other resources available for finding legislative information relevant to specific areas.

The content and suggestions in the Recommendations sections of this book fully reflect and support inclusive programming wherever possible and/or suitable. We believe that it is extremely important that educators of young children become more involved in working closely and dialoging with parents and specialists through observing, recording, and evaluating the behavior of the children in their group.

Teachers of young children have important contributions to make toward the assessment process. With education and child care budgets being strained to the limit in many places, it becomes crucial that those working with young children have skills and tools to support them in accurately evaluating, programming, and working effectively with children who have special needs. It is also important that early childhood professionals know how to access

- support agencies.

- medical specialists.

- government funding.

- special education benefits
- support groups for parents.

Initial interaction with parents of a child with previously unidentified special needs must be done with sensitivity and care. It is important for teachers of young children to realize that it is often difficult for parents to accept the fact that their child might have special needs. For this reason, it is especially important that teachers, when talking with parents of children who are presenting with problematic development and/or behavior, and who have not been previously diagnosed, be supportive and empathetic, and that care be given as to how they express their concern.

It is usually best to observe the following suggestions:

- First ask the parents about their observations and concerns with regard to their child's behavior and/or development. Frequently, parents have had concerns and may be unaware of where to turn for help. Other parents may be defensive and have trouble facing the fact that there may be something wrong with their child.

- It is also helpful to reassure the parents that the observed problem may be caused by a temporary delay, or may be something that has a medical basis that might be able to be treated and cured (especially true with hearing, vision, and so on).

- It is also useful to say something like, "The staff are unsure of how to most effectively meet your child's needs, but the sooner specialized support is obtained, the sooner we can program in the most effective ways for your child."

- Next, the teacher should recommend to the parents that they have a pediatrician examine the child. Parents should be asked to give written permission for the center to communicate and/or meet with the pediatrician. The center should also request that the parents obtain and share the pediatrician's written report.

- The center should ask the parents to give written permission for your local specialist (physiotherapist, psychologist, child interventionist, and so on) to observe and advise staff and/or the parents on how to most effectively interact with the child.

Note: Parental consent should be obtained in writing if teachers from a center/school/program wish to consult directly with and/or share information with a physician or outside agency that may be involved with a child.

RESOURCES FOR ADDITIONAL INFORMATION

Resources vary in different communities. In most areas you can find a public health official/nurse, a pediatrician, university medical centers, and/or other agencies that have information on where to turn for specialized support services. Child care centers and educational settings serving areas where inadequate services are available must advocate for additional support systems for parents, schools, and centers that have responsibility for young children with special needs. They should also learn how to most effectively access and evaluate material available on the Internet.

At the end of each section of the book, major organizations for each condition are included. Space has also been left for centers to record local agencies, specialists, and phone numbers.

BASIC PHILOSOPHY OF THE AUTHORS

Assessing and programming are ongoing processes that are technically never finished. The more that early childhood specialists are involved in the evaluation process, the better able they are to make necessary and appropriate program modifications to meet the specific needs of the child.

Be sure to remember that each child is first a child. Recognize the special needs, but try not to ever forget the uniqueness and individuality of the child as a person with feelings and awareness, and needs to be treated with care and dignity. Never forget that teachers are the model for ways of interacting with the child. Other children will observe and follow teachers' example.

It is the intent of this book to help you, the child's primary professional advocate, to participate more actively and comprehensively in the important process of identification, intervention, and inclusion of the child with special needs.

This book is a totally new and updated edition of an original text that was published by Addison Wesley in 1990. The content in all sections has been extensively revised and updated and a number of new sections and topics have been added. For those who are familiar with the original edition, there are now totally new sections on

- Anaphylactic Reaction
- Fetal Alcohol Syndrome (FAS)/Fetal Alcohol Effect (FAE)/Maternal Substance Abuse
- Post-Traumatic Stress Disorder (PTSD)
- Sickle Cell Anemia/Disease
- Tourette Syndrome and Behavioral Tics
- Traumatic Brain Injury (TBI)

Major revisions and expanded information have been included in the sections on

- AIDS (HIV-AIDS) (new scientific findings).
- Allergies–now includes information on Anaphylactic reaction.
- Arthritis–now includes information on Aspirin reaction.
- Autism Spectrum Disorder–now includes information on Asperger's Syndrome (Disorder), Rett Syndrome, Childhood Disintegrative Disorder, and Pervasive Developmental Disorder Not Otherwise Specified.
- Behavioral/Social/Emotional Problems–now includes Oppositional Defiant Disorder (ODD) and Elective/Selective Mutism.
- Cerebral Palsy–Augmentative Communication Systems has been totally revised.
- Intellectual Disabilities–now includes specific information on Down Syndrome, Fragile X Syndrome, Prader-Willi Syndrome, and Cri du Chat Syndrome.
- Learning Disabilities–now includes an expanded section on Sensory Integration Dysfunction.

This edition also includes major and easy-to-navigate Web sites for each section.

The authors and Delmar Learning affirm that the Web site URLs referenced herein were accurate at the time of printing. However, due to the fluid nature of the Internet, we cannot guarantee their accuracy for the life of the edition.

HOW TO USE THIS BOOK

1. All conditions/special needs included in this book are listed in the index in alphabetical order.

2. We urge the reader to think in terms of clusters of physical/behavioral symptoms, to realize that one symptom can be found in many different areas of special need, and to also take into consideration that no one case has all of the symptoms/behaviors that are listed.

3. When you check a specific section, Column 1 (the left column) lists all relevant Physical, Behavioral, Social/Emotional Characteristics that might be applicable to a certain condition.

4. Column 2 (the center column), in most instances, has Alternative Considerations and Conditions. These are lined up as closely as possible to be parallel to the specific behavioral/physical/social/emotional characteristics in Column 1. It is in Column 2 that we are trying to let the reader know that one symptom alone can be indicative of many different conditions.

5. In Column 2, **bold print** is used to indicate conditions that are found in the Index and expanded on in other sections. Column 2 also includes Essential Information and Important Questions to Ask. This information is provided in situations in which the condition under consideration will almost always have come to your center prediagnosed. (***Note:*** To conserve space, Important Questions to Ask occasionally appears in Column 1.)

6. Column 3 (the right-hand column) indicates Recommendations–programming suggestions, specific techniques, and strategies that might help in focusing and supporting a child with a special need; as well as recommendations on strategies to try out and program ideas to explore until someone with special qualifications can advise staff on ways of handling the specific needs of the child in question. We hope that some of the strategies indicated here will be of continued use after specific goals have been set for the child.

7. We have not attempted to line up Column 3 with Columns 1 and 2 as the material in Column 3 is relevant to all of the material in the other two columns.

    The specific strategies and programming ideas in Column 3 are conducive to the inclusion of a child with special needs in interacting with his/her chronological age group. We have sought to present programming ideas that will be of interest to, and support the development of *all* individuals in the group, as well as being of specific help to the child who has hypothesized special needs.

8. Throughout this book, we have used the terms "teachers," "staff," and "child caretakers" interchangeably.

9. **IT IS IMPORTANT TO REMEMBER THAT WE ARE <u>NOT</u> TRYING TO TURN TEACHERS OF YOUNG CHILDREN INTO DIAGNOSTICIANS. This book is to be used as a reference guide only, not as a medical manual.**

10. We urge teachers to take steps to obtain help for the child as soon as they observe behaviors about which they have concern. In order to do this, teachers must

- first approach the parents to discuss their concerns, find out what the parents have experienced, and then encourage the parents to seek professional diagnosis.

- obtain written parental permission for the center to seek special support services for the child and communicate with any specialist working with the child. (***Note:*** Parental permission is a requirement in almost all areas of the United States and Canada.)

- set up some type of system whereby ongoing dialogue between the parents and the center can be maintained.

It is through working as a team—home, school, child care center, and health care providers—with shared goals and strategies, that the most success in helping a child to reach his/her greatest potential can be achieved.

ABOUT THE AUTHORS

Carol L. Paasche was a Professor and Coordinator of Early Childhood Education at Seneca College, Toronto, Ontario, for 30 years. She received her Master of Education degree in guidance and counseling from Harvard University, and has done additional doctoral studies in research and children with special needs at the University of Michigan. She has certification in primary education, early childhood education, and counseling, and has worked in programs for young children in New York, Ohio, and Michigan. She was instrumental in setting up over 30 part-time Head Start–type inclusive readiness programs in the Toronto area. She has taught a range of subjects, including child development, children with special needs, assessing through observing, curriculum, sociology of the family, and interpersonal communications. In the course of her responsibilities as Coordinator of Field Placement, she visited hundreds of preschool centers, child care centers, and kindergartens throughout Metropolitan Toronto and the surrounding area.

Mrs. Paasche is coauthor of *Inclusion in Early Childhood Programs: Children with Exceptionalities* (Thomson/Nelson, 2002). She currently is a consultant on children with special needs to a number of early childhood centers and has a parent and child counseling practice.

Lola Gorrill was Head of Educational Services at Adventure Place, a mental health center for young children and their families. Her responsibilities included assessment, programming, and evaluation of children with special needs. Her role included consulting with teacher/therapists and families to plan individualized educational programs for each child. She holds a Bachelor's degree in Psychology from York University; Primary, Junior, and Intermediate teaching certificates; as well as Specialist qualifications in Primary (pre-kindergarten through grade 3) and Special Education. Prior to specializing in special education, she taught in the primary grades for ten years.

Ms. Gorrill was part of a transdisciplinary team, including teachers, child care staff, speech and language pathologist, psychologists, and social workers that was responsible for the assessments and programming for children with special needs. Her role also included consulting with teacher/therapists and families to plan individualized educational program plans for the children in the center.

She is a founding member of the Autistic Society in Ontario, Canada and is the parent of an adult with autism.

Bev Strom has a diploma in Early Childhood Education from Seneca College. She has worked as a consultant to preschool centers, advising teachers on ways of programming for children with behavioral and developmental problems. Part of her work consisted of providing individual program plans for children in treatment, as well as adapting recommendations from clinical staff into methodology compatible with preschool programs.

ACKNOWLEDGMENTS

We express our appreciation to the many people who have supported, assisted, and encouraged us. Special thanks go to those who served on the North York Inter-Agency Preschool Sub-Committee, the staff of Adventure Place, the Early Childhood Education Department of Seneca College, North York General Hospital, Community and Social Services Program Advisors, frontline teachers, as well as all those who reviewed this text and offered us valuable feedback and suggestions.

We are particularly indebted to the late Dr. Milton I. Levine who was editor of the Pediatric Annals and Professor Emeritus of Cornell Medical School, as well as other medical and public health personnel who edited and made suggestions on the medical portions of the book.

We need to express our indebtedness to our families and friends who provided patience and support throughout the writing of the book.

We also thank the following reviewers, enlisted by Delmar Learning, for their helpful suggestions and constructive criticism:

Marie Brand
State University of New York–New Paltz
New Paltz, NY

Ruth Halo
Middlesex County Economic Opportunities Corporation
   (Head Start)
North Brunswick, NJ

Sandra Hughes
Rainbow Express Child Care Center
Schenectady, NY

Jennifer Johnson
Vance-Granville Community College
Henderson, NC

Linda Rivers
Signal Centers
Chattanooga, TN

Brenda Schin
Private Child Care Provider
Ballston Spa, NY

Sarah Snyder
Capital District Beginnings, Inc.
Troy, NY

Tracy Walzcak
Orfordville School District
Orfordville, WI

ABUSE/NEGLECT
(Child Abuse/Neglect)

Child Abuse/Neglect—Child abuse is the term used to describe physical, emotional, and sexual abuse, as well as neglect. The child may be subject to physical harm, sexual molestation, emotional maltreatment, or any and all of the these.

Child Neglect is the failure of the parent/caregiver to provide adequate physical, emotional, and social care, nutrition (food), health care, education, shelter, clothing, and/or personal protection.

PHYSICAL AND EMOTIONAL ABUSE OR NEGLECT

BEHAVIORAL CHARACTERISTICS	Alternative Considerations and Conditions	Recommendations
The child may 1. be unusually aggressive, disruptive, or destructive (toward peers or self). 2. be unusually fearful or withdrawn. 3. be passive and/or overly compliant. 4. be irritable and/or anxious. 5. be listless, detached, or depressed. 6. be suffering from poor self-esteem. 7. demand an unusual amount of physical contact and/or attention. 8. show no affection or emotion. 9. show no separation anxiety. 10. have a poor sense of safety. 11. be unable to differentiate fantasy from reality. 12. be compulsively neat and tidy. 13. be compulsively "good," e.g. always helping, or overly precise in following rules.	**Behavioral/Social/Emotional Problems** **Autism Spectrum Disorder** **Intellectual Disabilities**	• Observe and record any questionable behavior or physical problem. • Observe parent/child interaction. • Encourage play with peers; implement small-group play. • Praise and encourage the child's efforts in all areas, offering extra support when needed. • Set health and safety limits. • Encourage messy activities, like finger-painting, water and sand play. • Include regular health checkups as part of the ongoing program. • Record the location of any physical injury or deviation in physical condition; be sure to give explicit description, date and time of observation, and sign the statement. Contact the supervisor of the program, and then make sure this incident is reported to a child protection agency if there is any possibility of abuse and/or neglect.

14. admit to being punished, does not want the suspected abuser to be contacted.

15. be worried about removing clothing for gym activities, medical help, or physical examination.

16. be verbally abusive toward peers or self—e.g., "I'm stupid," "You're ugly."

17. resort to repetitive behavior, such as rocking, twirling hair, and so on.

18. avoid eye contact.

19. have a compelling need to take objects from peers or the center.

20. reflect overall poor physical care (see Physical Characteristics).

21. back off when approached or touched.

22. have poor attention/poor concentration.

23. have poor social relationships with peers.

24. have inconsistent attendance, early or late arrival and/or pickup from center.

25. demonstrate behavior in the center that differs from that which is reported by the parents.

26. have delays or sudden regression in speech and language; concept development; adaptive behavior; fine and gross motor development.

27. fear or resist going home.

Cultural Influences/English as a Second Language/English with a Dialect

Autism Spectrum Disorder
Cultural Influences/English as a Second Language/English with a Dialect

Fears from previous experiences

Intellectual Disabilities
Attention Deficit/Hyperactive Disorder

Speech and Language Problems
Visual Impairment
Hearing Impairment
Cultural Influences/English as a Second Language/English with a Dialect
Developmental delays
Behavioral/Social/Emotional Problems

- Encourage dramatic play—two to three children plus the teacher participating and/or facilitating—to foster social/-emotional expression.

Remember: The source of abuse may be siblings, other relatives, a caregiver, sitter, neighbors, as well as one or both parents. The parents may/may not be aware of the problem.

PHYSICAL CHARACTERISTICS

The child may

1. have unusual and/or unexplained burns; bruises; marks on face, back, buttocks, trunk (usually at different stages of healing).

2. be dressed inappropriately and/or wear clothing to cover injuries, even in hot weather.

3. have fractures.

4. be fatigued or lethargic.

5. appear ill.

6. be pale.

7. lack medical/dental care.

8. have bald patches on scalp.

9. be unwashed.

10. appear to be constantly hungry or have loss of appetite.

11. have abdominal pain and/or headaches.

12. be underweight.

Cultural Influences/English as a Second Language/English with a Dialect

Could be caused by worms, vitamin deficiency, food allergy, or sensitivity to food

Failure to Thrive
Nutritional Deficiencies

- Do not single out the child in front of other children.

- Observe/examine the child as unobtrusively as possible.

- Make the environment as comfortable and supportive as possible for the child.

- Make sure extra garments are available so that the child is not excluded from outdoor play and other activities if his/her clothing is inappropriate for the situation.

SEXUAL ABUSE

BEHAVIORAL CHARACTERISTICS

The child may

1. display sexual knowledge/interest beyond his/her developmental level through actions, verbal comments, and/or drawing sexually explicit pictures.

2. display regressive behavior, such as bed-wetting, thumb-sucking.

3. have a sudden onset of unaccountable nightmares, fears, and phobias, such as the dark, loud noises, males, babysitters, and so on.

4. be unwilling to participate in physical activities, which demand removal of clothing, such as gym.

5. have noticeable changes in personality, such as withdrawal, depression, poor social skills, behavior that is insecure (e.g., clinging), and/or overreacting to discipline.

6. try to be perfect and be very insecure about his/her achievements.

7. be unable to concentrate on tasks.

8. have a loss of appetite or compulsive eating.

9. have difficulty maintaining peer relationships.

10. have a history of self-inflicted injuries.

May be a response to the birth of a new sibling or other change in the family situation

May be shyness; may have had little previous experience in this type of situation

Behavioral/Social/Emotional Problems

- Check to see whether the child gains weight a short time after entering the program.

- Keep an ongoing record of the child's behavior and comments.

- Try not to "make a big thing" out of something the child does or says, but be sure to keep a written (dated and signed) record of the incident.

- If a child is uncomfortable or in pain, do not press for him/her to do the undesired activity. *Do* record the incident.

Remember: Be sure to record (with date and signature) any behaviors or conditions that you feel may be indicators of possible abuse or neglect.

PHYSICAL CHARACTERISTICS

The child may

1. have difficulty sitting or walking.

2. have swelling, itching, or pain in the genital area.

May be a consequence of masturbation

3. have bleeding or lacerations of external genitalia.

4. have pain when urinating.

Kidney and Bladder Disorders
Other medical condition
May be from constipation

5. have stained, torn, or bloody underclothing.

6. have vaginal/penile discharge or infection.

May be due to a vaginal/penile infection

7. have constant sore throat of unknown origin

Allergies

REPORTING RESPONSIBILITIES

Note: In the United States and Canada, teachers and medical professionals are legally required to report suspected cases of child abuse. Any professional person who fails to report suspected abuse may be fined up to $10,000 and face imprisonment. The Child Protective Service (CPS), which is part of the police department, will investigate the reports. Check your state/province to find out local agencies and any specific regulations in your area for reporting child abuse.

In Canada, all suspected cases of abuse must be reported to Child and Family Service Organizations. The Child and Family Services Act (CFSA s.72(1) states: "If a person has reasonable grounds to suspect that a child is or may be in need of protection, the person must promptly report the suspicion and the information upon which it is based to a children's aid society."

Any professional or official who fails to report a suspicion that a child is or may be in need of protection, where the information on which that suspicion is based was obtained in the course of his or her professional or official duties, is liable on conviction to a serious fine.

RESOURCES

LOCAL

Child Welfare Office (USA)
Child and Family Services (Canada)

Public Health Officials

Medical services (clinics, hospitals)

Help line (phone numbers)

Parents' Anonymous organization
Local address: _____

_____

_____

Phone number: _____

UNITED STATES

National Clearing House on Child Abuse and
  Neglect
330 C Street SW
Washington, DC 20447
Tel: 1-800-394-3366
Online: http://www.calib.com

Child Protective Services
For state telephone number listings:
 Child Help USA National Abuse Hotline
 Tel: 1-800-422-4453
 Online: http://www.acf.dhhs.gov

CANADA

National Clearing House on Family Violence
Jeanne Mance Building
Postal Locator 1907D1
Tunney's Pasture
Ottawa, Ontario K1A 1B4
Tel: 1-800-267-1291
Online: http://www.hc-sc.gc.ca

Ministry of Community Family and Children's
  Services
Online: http://www.gov.on.ca

Children's Aid Society; Catholic Children's Aid
  Society–Check your local listing

ADDITIONAL RESOURCES

_____

_____

_____

_____

_____

_____

_____

_____

_____

_____

ALLERGIES

Allergies are abnormal reactions of the body's immune system to certain substances called allergens. In most people, the substance does not produce any physical symptoms. In a susceptible person, it triggers an allergic reaction. The symptoms can be severe or mild. The tendency to be allergic is frequently inherited. A child may or may not be prediagnosed when he/she comes to your center.

Note: If a child has a prediagnosed history of an allergy, a specific list of allergies, or a condition caused by an allergy such as hay fever, keep the information of specific triggers handy. Be aware of the nature of the allergic reaction and the recommended treatment. The child's medication and physician's name and phone number should be readily available. An emergency number for the parents and/or parent substitute should also be available.

PHYSICAL AND BEHAVIORAL CHARACTERISTICS	Alternative Considerations and Conditions	Recommendations
1. Skin The child may be itchy and have • red blotches. • hives (white lumps with red inflamed areas). • eczema (red, inflamed, itchy rash).	Childhood diseases–German measles; measles; roseola; chicken pox	• A list indicating the child's name and known allergies should be posted in a place where substitute teachers and participating parents are required to check. • Refer for medical checkup if symptoms are interfering with the child's ability to participate. • Look for possible causes (triggers) in the school environment.
2. Respiratory System The child may have • runny, itchy, red, swollen eyes. • dark circles under the eyes. • stuffy and/or runny nose; tends to rub nose upward with palm of hand, to increase intake of air. • ears that itch or feel clogged. • shortness of breath. • mouth breathing, sneezing, drooling, snoring, snorting, wheezing. • itchy mouth and/or throat.	Simple cold Tonsil/adenoid infections Respiratory infection **Asthma**	• Try to record when/where and possible cause of allergic reaction. • Try to note any pattern of the attacks. • If the child should become upset, or have a fairly severe allergic reaction, try to remain calm; be accepting, but don't make a big issue over it. Try to make the child feel relaxed and comfortable. • Remove the possible cause from the child's environment as soon as possible. • Encourage use of a Medic Alert bracelet for those suffering from a severe allergy.

- swelling of the lips, mouth, throat, and/or tongue.
- frequent coughing (tendency toward croup).

3. Stomach (Digestion Process)

The child may have

- nausea and or/vomiting.
- stomach cramps/indigestion.
- constipation or diarrhea (which may contain blood or mucus).

4. Other overall reactions include:

- unexplained fevers.
- excessive sweating.
- hyperventilating.
- general feeling of illness–weight fluctuations.
- headaches.
- irritability, shortness of temper, frequent crying.
- poor appetite.
- fatigue.

Tension and stress may lead to headaches, stomach cramps, constipation/diarrhea, and other physical reactions.

Note: Many Asian and African children cannot tolerate cow's milk. The parents may not be aware of this until they are living in North America. Even then, they may not be aware that it is the milk which is creating digestive problems in their child.

Behavioral/Social/Emotional Problems

Cystic Fibrosis
Diabetes

Weight fluctuations, feelings of weakness and dizziness may be caused by metabolic or glandular problems.

Some children who have changed their climate and diet and are unaccustomed to the "dry" heat of indoors and severe cold of outdoors in winter.

- Beware of products containing latex, as many children are now reacting to these. Latex products can be
  –balloons
  –rubber bands
  –bandaids
  –latex paint
  –pacifiers, bottle nipples

Anaphylactic Reaction

A child with a previous history of **Anaphylactic Reaction** (a severe, life-threatening allergic reaction) could be "at risk" for another severe reaction.

Symptoms of an anaphylactic reaction may include:

- a tingling or warm sensation.
- hives.
- wheezing or difficulty breathing.
- vomiting.
- diarrhea.

Symptoms may occur from 5 to 45 minutes and up to 2 hours after exposure to the allergen. Check with the child's parents.

For a child with a known anaphylactic reaction, the *EPIPEN@Jr.* should be in the center and all staff should be taught how to use it.

POSSIBLE CAUSES (TRIGGERS) OF ALLERGIC REACTION

1. Airborne
- pollens (plants and trees)
- molds, (often in the air; frequently in older houses or damp basements)
- fur, animal dander, and saliva
- dust mites, cockroaches
- feathers (e.g., pillows)
- house dust
- tobacco smoke
- chalk dust
- perfume

2. Foods, especially
- eggs
- milk
- chocolate
- shellfish
- fruits–e.g., oranges, strawberries
- tree nuts
- peanuts
- soy
- tomatoes
- wheat products

3. Medicines
- aspirin
- Penicillin
- sulfa drugs

4. Weather
- very hot or very cold temperature
- very dry or very moist air
- over exposure to the sun
- sudden changes in weather

5. Insect stings, especially
- bees
- black flies

6. Contact with certain
- plants
- cosmetics
- dyes (often found in paints and other chemicals)
- fabric material (e.g., wool)
- hand or laundry soap
- clay may dry and irritate overly sensitive skin
- latex products (rubber gloves; certain toys; and so on)

7. Bacterial or Viral Illnesses
- At times other illnesses (i.e. respiratory conditions such as colds) and/or medication will trigger allergic reactions.

ALLERGIES VERSUS FOOD INTOLERANCE

Food Intolerance
In food allergies, it is the immune system that reacts inappropriately to a specific food. Food intolerance differs from food allergies in that the cause is frequently unknown. Identifiable causes, such as an enzyme deficiency, are at times found.

Lactose intolerance–the child is unable to digest the lactose (natural sugar) in milk.

Celiac disease–the child reacts to gluten (starches and wheat products) and is unable to effectively digest them.

RESOURCES

LOCAL

Allergy associations and societies

Allergy clinics in all major hospitals

Physicians who specialize in allergies (allergists)
or in allergic skin reactions (dermatologists)

Local hospital or university clinics

Medic Alert bracelet information

UNITED STATES

American Academy of Allergy Asthma
  Immunology
611 East Wells Street
Milwaukee, WI 53202
Tel: 1-800-822-2762
Online: http://www.aaaai.org

American Latex Allergy Association
  (A.L.E.R.T. Inc.)
P.O. Box 13930
Milwaukee, WI 53213-0930
Tel: 1-888-97ALERT
Online: http://www.latexallergyresources.org

The Food Allergy and Anaphylaxis Network
10400 Eaton Place, Suite 107
Fairfax, VA 22030-2208
Tel: 1-800-929-4040
Online: http://www.foodallergy.org

CANADA

Canadian Society of Allergy and Clinical
  Immunology
774 Echo Drive
Ottawa, Ontario K1S 5N8
Tel: 1-613-730-8177
Online: http://www.csaci.medical.org

Anaphylaxis Canada
416 Moore Avenue, Suite 306
Toronto, Ontario M4G 1C9
Tel: 1-416-785-5666
Online: http://www.anaphylaxis.org

ADDITIONAL RESOURCES

AMPUTATIONS/BORN WITHOUT LIMBS

Amputations refer to children who have been born without a limb, as well as those who have lost a limb in an accident, or have had one removed for medical reasons.

PHYSICAL AND BEHAVIORAL CHARACTERISTICS

1. The greater the number of joints that are missing, the more difficult the adjustment for the child.

2. The level of adjustment is related to the age at which this occurred–the earlier the loss, the more likely that the child will have adjusted.

3. The more supportive, accepting, and encouraging the parents and teachers are toward the child, the more likely the child is able to cope effectively with the impairment.

4. Prosthetic devices are almost always available. How well these fit, how functional they are, the child's attitude toward them, and how easily the child can manage them are all factors of which the center needs to be aware.

5. It is important to know the child's level of competence with/without the prosthetic device. Some children have adjusted to functioning without the device, but could do much more if they learned to function adequately with it. Some devices are more cosmetic than functional.

Essential Information

Be sure to get a history as to how long and under what circumstances the child has lost the limb. This will help staff to know the possible psychological effects this may be having on the child.

Children who lose a limb after the age of two may experience the "phantom limb" sensation. This means that the child may feel as if the missing limb is still present; may experience sensation, possibly itching or pain, even though no limb is present.

Important Questions to Ask

What agency or person can be contacted for advice?

How are prosthetic devices, limbs, put on and/or adjusted?

How often and under what circumstances should the prosthetic device be removed? Should the child have a choice with regard to removing a prosthesis?

What activities, if any, should be avoided because they might hurt the child and/or be harmful to the prosthetic limb?

Recommendations

- It is important to obtain a list of appropriate activities from the child's therapist. It is then up to the teachers to adapt these ideas so that others in the group can participate, and the child then can become a participating member.

- Work to develop activities that improve self-help skills, build on social skills, and self-esteem.

- Adapting the position of a toy or the height at which something can be used (raising or lowering a table or easel) often makes it possible for the child to participate more fully.

- Bicycles and other outdoor wheel toys may need to be adapted–for example, by using Velcro straps, a specially constructed seat, and so on, to enable a child with a functional or nonfunctional limb to be able to position him- or herself more securely.

- Try not to make a big thing of the missing limb/s. Accept this child as equally as possible with the other children. Remember, staff attitudes and actions provide a model for the children of how to act appropriately.

- If the child who is missing a limb has no access to any special agencies, a local health official should be alerted.

Note: See **Cerebral Palsy** and **Spina Bifida** for additional recommendations.

RESOURCES

LOCAL

Thalidomide organizations that can give information on other resources

War amputations and other organizations and hospitals that may have information on prosthetic limbs

University departments of rehabilitation

Medical research foundations

Amputee societies

Children's orthopedic centers

Hospitals that have clinical services for children born without limbs, as well as those who lost limbs due to illness

UNITED STATES

Amputee Coalition of America
900 East Hill Avenue, Suite 285
Knoxville, Tennessee 37915-2568
Tel: 1-888-267-5669
Online: http://www.amputee-coalition.org

March of Dimes/Birth Defects Foundation (US)
1275 Mamaroneck Avenue
White Plains, New York 10606
Online: http://www.modimes.org

CANADA

War Amps of Canada
2827 Riverside Drive
Ottawa, Ontario K1V 0C4
Tel: 1-877-622-2472
Online: http://www.waramps.ca

Easter Seals/March of Dimes National Council
90 Eglinton Avenue East, Suite 511
Toronto, Ontario M4P 2Y3
Tel: 416-932-8382
Online: http://www.esmodnc.org

ADDITIONAL RESOURCES

ARTHRITIS
(Juvenile Arthritis)

Juvenile Arthritis is a noncontagious condition that causes swelling and/or inflammation of the joint linings, resulting in pain in one or more joints. It is exhibited in a number of different ways. However, there are some basic characteristics that are usually evident in one form or another in all types.

Juvenile arthritis differs from arthritis found in people over 16 years of age in that there is an excellent chance that with proper treatment and physiotherapy, after a period of months or years there will be total remission with no remaining serious disabilities evident. The main treatment used is high dosages of aspirin or ibuprofen for temporary relief of swelling, pain, and stiffness.

Though most children who have juvenile arthritis will come to your center prediagnosed, it is also possible that you may be the first to recognize a cluster of physical characteristics that may indicate the onset of this condition.

PHYSICAL CHARACTERISTICS	Alternative Considerations and Conditions	Recommendations

The child may
 	
1. experience recurrent and persistent pain, swelling, stiffness of any joints—legs, wrists, hands, neck, and lower back.
 	
2. experience pain and stiffness that are most severe first thing in the morning and may be worse on some days than on others.
 	
3. experience stiffness of the joints, which often leads to weakness of the muscles around the joints. This occurs most often when there is lack of movement for a long period of time.
 	
4. have skin that at times becomes red in the area of "arthritic" joints.
 	
5. appear listless, weak, pale, or have loss of weight.
	Muscular Dystrophy
	
	Rheumatic fever
	
	Pulled muscles/bruises
	
	Abuse/Neglect
	
	Lupus (erythematosus) (usually found in teenagers and adults)
	
	Anemia
	Leukemia
		• It is important to treat this child as much like his/her peers as possible, expecting the child to follow the same routines and limits as other children in the group, while at the same time taking into consideration any special conditions that are required because of his/her arthritis. These may include:
		
		   –allowing the child extra time to get from one place to another.
		
		   –allowing periods of rest between active physical activity if the child indicates he/she needs them.
		
		Other recommendations include:
		
		• If a problem is suspected, it is important to consult with the child's parents and/or physician.
		
		• Children with arthritis may have great fluctuations in how they feel from one day to the next. Try to be sensitive to this.

6. have frequent high fevers. The child's temperature may fluctuate up and down in a single day. This may last for a number of weeks, but rarely more than six months.

7. have chills and shaking, often accompanied by a fever.

8. have a rash that comes and goes for many days, usually occurring at the time of a fever; in some cases the child may have psoriasis as a co-condition.

9. experience abdominal pain.

10. have eye inflammation.

11. have inflammation of the joints, which may speed up or slow down growth centers in the bones; therefore, some bones may be longer or shorter than normal.

12. have enlarged lymph nodes (glands in the neck and under arms are often swollen).

BEHAVIORAL CHARACTERISTICS

The child may

1. not want to use an arm or leg because of pain.

2. walk with a limp.

3. be irritable because of pain; may want to avoid some activities (should not be forced to do them).

Nutritional Deficiencies

Allergies

Cystic Fibrosis

Eye infection

Child may have inherited body proportions that slow him/her down.

Abuse/Neglect
Pulled muscles

Muscular Dystrophy

- Exercise in a warm pool is also helpful. Is there a pool available to the center for all the children to use?

- The child should participate in whatever activity, exercise, and/or play that his/her physical condition may allow.

- Any activity that will help to build the child's self-esteem is especially important. It is important to think of what the child is able to do and not to focus on his/her limitations.

4. need periods of rest between activities.

5. have developed emotional/social difficulties as a consequence of family stress and/or lack of previous experience with other children.

Nutritional Deficiencies
Anemia
Lack of sleep

IMPORTANT QUESTIONS TO ASK

Essential Information

Does the child need to wear splints of any kind? If yes, how often? How are they attached and adjusted?

Is the child on any medication? If yes, what kind?

Are there any medical side effects to watch for?

How often must he/she take medication and how/when must it be administered?

Are eyedrops required? How often? How should they be administered?

Are there any activity restrictions? If yes, what are they? What symptoms should be watched for?

Are there any required physical activities? If yes, what types of things are recommended?

Note: Most children with arthritis need to have ongoing periods of activity throughout the day in order to avoid stiffness. Staff should try to find out what the optimal timing is.

For your information: Typical signs of a reaction to too much aspirin are
- rapid or deep breathing.
- ringing in the ears.
- drowsiness.
- nausea.
- vomiting.
- irritability.
- unusual behavior.

- The therapist or physician might be able to suggest some activities that are particularly useful for this child and that can be incorporated into group activities for all the children.

- Medical information, such as "extra rest" or "drug reaction," should be written and posted where all staff can have access to it.

- The center should have a written statement from the child's physician as to what specific procedures to follow.

- Be sure that all staff are aware of the special needs for this child.

- The child should be wearing a Medic Alert bracelet.

- If any symptoms listed are noted, the parents should be notified.

- It should be previously established what procedures are to be followed if any possible reactions to medication occur.

Note: If there is a stomach flu or viral infection "going around" the center, one might conclude that it is a reaction to his/her medication, when in fact this child has the same infection the other children have.

RESOURCES

LOCAL

Arthritis foundations and societies

Occupational therapy clinics/hospital services

Physiotherapy clinics

UNITED STATES

Arthritis Foundation
P.O. Box 7669
Atlanta, GA 30357-0669
Tel: 1-800-283-7800
Online: http://www.arthritis.org

International Stills Disease Foundation Inc.
1123 S. Kimbrel Avenue
Panama City, FL 32404
Online: http://www.stillsdisease.org

World Orthopedics
Online: http://www.worldortho.com

CANADA

The Arthritis Society
National Office
393 University Avenue, Suite 1700
Toronto, Ontario M5G 1E6
Tel: 1-416-979-7228
Online: http://www.arthritis.ca

Canadian Arthritis Network
Online: http://www.arthritisnetwork.ca

ADDITIONAL RESOURCES

ASTHMA

Asthma is a chronic respiratory condition that at times causes a narrowing of the bronchial tubes. As the lining of the airways becomes swollen and inflamed, it may induce the formation of excess mucus, which in turn may block the smaller airways. An allergic reaction results when the bronchial mucous membrane becomes irritated, due to an inhaled or absorbed irritant, such as insect bites, bee stings, food, or a virus.

Asthma is the most common respiratory condition found in young children.

The child with asthma will have repeated episodes of breathing difficulty. It often sounds like he/she is gasping for air.

Note: A child may come to your center prediagnosed as having asthma. It is important to know of any medication the child may be taking or may need to take. Find out what known things may trigger an asthma attack; what physical limitations, if any exist?

Be sure to know whom to contact in case of an asthma attack that you are unable to bring under control.

PHYSICAL AND BEHAVIORAL CHARACTERISTICS	Alternative Considerations and Conditions	Recommendations
The child may 1. have an irritating, dry cough. 2. experience mild wheezing. 3. have eczema, hives, hay fever, or itchy eyes. 4. have diagnosed allergies that in turn may trigger the asthma. 5. have heartburn, belching, spitting up (in infants). 6. be small and pale. 7. be overweight through lack of exercise. 8. have behavioral problems resulting from these physical characteristics. 9. have fatigue due to lack of sleep.	May be a respiratory infection or temporary irritation of the bronchial tubes An obstruction that might have narrowed the trachea (windpipe)	• Remain relaxed and accepting. • Involve the child in a quiet, nonstressful activity until the symptoms are relieved. • If the child's condition is questioned by other children, explain that sometimes this child has a little trouble breathing, but that it is temporary and will not last long. • Do not make the child eat if he/she does not feel up to it. • Give many opportunities for success in what the child does well; work on building social/peer relationships. • Rest periods should be built into the regular physical activity program.

10. exhibit drug-produced side effects (nervousness, restlessness, heart palpitations, nausea, rapid pulse, sweating, drowsiness, agitation).

Causes ("Triggers")

1. Viral infections, e.g., common colds, sinus infections with post nasal drip.

2. Excessive activity, e.g., running, laughing, and so on.

3. Emotional stress and anxiety may provoke or make an asthma attack more severe.

4. Sudden changes in indoor temperature; very dry or wet; very hot or cold. Outdoors: cold, damp, or dry air.

5. Allergens and irritants:

   - Animals: cockroaches, household pets (dander and saliva from dogs, cats, rabbits, and gerbils).

   - Food: at times, juice, milk, nuts, eggs, peanuts, peanut butter, chocolate, fish, whole wheat, seafood.

   - Airborne: house dust, dust mites, chalk dust, talcum powder, candle smoke, feathers, wool, grasses, pollens, and molds.

   - Odors: perfume, scented soap, paint, tobacco smoke, cosmetics, car exhaust fumes, cooking fumes, spices, cleansers, and so on.

   - Chemical cleaning products.

Allergies

- Check the environment for any known triggers for allergies and try to determine whether something in the environment may be causing the problem, such as animals in the center, foods being served, smog, room dust or chalk dust, plant pollen, perfume, or cigarette smoke.

- If staff have any ideas of what might be triggering the attack, remove it from the environment or remove the child from the source.

- In a dry room, a humidifier or vaporizer may help by adding moisture to the air. In a damp room/area, a dehumidifier may help to eliminate moisture and molds.

- With parent approval, consult the child's physician for assistance in management of the child with asthma.

- Have an action plan in place for help in breathing methods to cope with an attack: use of drugs, a compressor, or bronchialdilator, nebulizer, or inhaler.

- Products containing latex (see allergies)
- Missed asthma medication

Note: Some medications trigger asthma. The child may have an allergic reaction to the product—e.g., aspirin, some antibiotics, and so on.

Note: Asthma may appear worse than it really is. If the child is wheezing but does not appear to be in distress, staff may allow the child to rest and play quietly for a few minutes and see whether his/her breathing improves.

It is always important to keep the child's medication for asthma available.

Allergies

RESOURCES

LOCAL

Local asthma and lung associations, societies, and foundations

Doctors specializing in allergies (allergists) and respiratory conditions

Local clinics/hospitals

UNITED STATES

Asthma and Allergy Foundation of America
1233 20th Street NW, Suite 402
Washington, DC 20036
Tel: 1-202-466-7643
Online: http://www.aaa.org

American Lung Association
61 Broadway, 6th Floor
New York, NY 10006
Tel: 1-212-315-8700
Online: http://www.lungusa.org

CANADA

Asthma Society of Canada
130 Bridgeland Avenue, Suite 425
Toronto, Ontario M6A 1Z4
Tel: 1-800-787-3880
Online: http://www.asthmasociety.ca

The Canadian Lung Association
573 King Street East, Suite 201
Toronto, Ontario M5A 4L3
Tel: 1-800-972-2636
Online: http://www.lung.ca

ADDITIONAL RESOURCES

ATTENTION DEFICIT/HYPERACTIVITY DISORDER
(ADHD and ADD)

Attention Deficit Disorder (ADD) is a developmental disorder characterized by a disability that interferes with the ability of the child to attend to a stimulus long enough to accomplish a task and/or receive information. If the child also exhibits hyperactive behaviors, it is referred to as **Attention Deficit Disorder with Hyperactivity (ADHD)**. ADHD is more common in boys, and ADD is more common in girls. The onset of this condition occurs during the early years. Some symptoms may persist into adulthood or disappear during puberty.

Note: Since other similar behavioral symptoms are common to other childhood disorders, it is important to make sure the child has had a thorough physical examination to first rule out a physical problem such as hearing, vision, or motor. Furthermore, other childhood disorders such as mood and behavioral disorders, and specific learning disabilities involving visual, auditory, and motor dysfunction, must be ruled out.

The exact cause is still unknown. Possible causes include: genetics, poor maternal nutrition, viral infections, maternal substance abuse, exposure to lead, traumatic brain injury, and neurological disorders of unknown origin. *It is not, as once popularly believed, due to poor parenting.*

Treatment: Psychosocial therapy and parental guidance, combined with carefully regulated medication, will help to lessen and often control ADHD and ADD symptoms.

HYPERACTIVITY

PHYSICAL AND BEHAVIORAL CHARACTERISTICS	Alternative Considerations and Conditions	Recommendations
The child 1. exhibits excessive motor activity. 2. exhibits frequent non–goal-directed activity. 3. has excessive movements that appear to be beyond his/her control. 4. cannot sit still, fidgets and squirms. 5. has many nonfunctional movements of parts of the body–grimacing, grinding teeth, sucking thumb. 6. runs and climbs rather than walks. 7. is always touching and experimenting-with little apparent learning taking place.	**Note:** Most children are active and energetic, but are able to direct their behavior in a productive manner. Children with ADD and/or those with ADHD are unable to do this. **Hearing Impairment** **Visual Impairment** Sensory deficits: children with hearing and/or vision problems often exhibit these types of behaviors. Emotional stress **Cerebral Palsy** **Autism Spectrum Disorder** **Tourette Syndrome (Disorder)** Other neurological disabilities Damage to the central nervous system Environmental stress	• Try to create an environment in which there is space that can be used often throughout the day for active movement, but that also has enclosed areas in which the child will be less easily distracted. • Use corners of rooms for different types of learning activities, including a quiet area that can be used for nonpunitive "calming down" or "cooling off" times. This area might have small blocks, small toys, and so on. • Try to minimize noise and visual distractions. Check to see whether background music calms and helps the child to focus or keeps the child from focusing.

8. requires little sleep. Excessive movement may be noticed during sleep.

9. is unable to play quietly.

10. is impatient.

INATTENTION

The child

1. has a short attention span, is easily distracted, is unable to concentrate.

2. is easily overstimulated by visual and auditory environments.

3. is unable to focus even on favorite tasks.

4. fails to listen, and therefore is unable to follow directions.

5. fails to complete tasks even when motivated to do so.

6. forgets daily routines.

7. may daydream.

8. is unable to organize and complete tasks.

9. is often easily bored.

IMPULSIVITY

The child

1. acts without thinking, often may over- or underreact or be unaware of possible consequences.

Family style of living may lack organization and/or support for learning.

Allergies
Prematurity/Preterm
Child is anemic–has iron deficiency.

Learning Disabilities
Sensory Integration Dysfunction
Delayed school readiness

Immature development

Lacks the ability to complete a task

Autism Spectrum Disorder
Intellectual Disabilities

Note: Children with metabolic, conduct, or affective disorders may exhibit similar behaviors.

- When the child is involved in nonfunctional behaviors (grimacing, tooth grinding, and so on), try to distract the child from the behavior and redirect him/her to some activity or interest center without calling attention to the behavior that one is trying to eliminate.

- Whenever possible, try to extend the amount of time a child is focused on some object or activity. Touching while talking about the object can help to do this.

- Get the child's attention before talking to him/her.

- Keep instructions simple.

- Keep directed activity periods short.

- Develop realistic expectations for the child.

- Arrange for the child to sit near the teacher during group activity times when he/she may have trouble attending or participating.

- Allow the child to hold an object in his/her hands, for example, when listening to a story.

- Limits: Rules and realistic consequences should be clearly stated and carried out consistently.

- Maintain daily routines as much as possible.

2. flits from one activity to another.

3. is unable to organize play and learning activities and/or routine tasks.

4. is often physically disruptive, requires frequent supervision.

5. has trouble taking turns; is unable to wait for his/her turn.

6. may talk constantly, but quality of conversation and comprehension may be poor.

7. verbally interrupts; calls out in group time.

8. may complete tasks quickly, but the quality is poor.

9. tends to give quick guesses rather than thinking through problems presented.

10. often displays poor judgment in social situations and personal safety situations.

EXCITABILITY

The child

1. is easily upset.

2. changes moods quickly.

3. is easily frustrated.

4. is irritable for no apparent reason.

5. can be aggressive and/or destructive when upset.

6. has temper tantrums.

Learning Disabilities

Behavioral/Social/Emotional Problems

Intellectual Disabilities

Behavioral/Social/Emotional Problems

- Positively reward the child with verbal or physical recognition whenever he/she is involved in a positive situation. Let the child know what a good job he/she has done–for example, "You put away all of your toys, that's great."

- Try to provide early intervention to avoid aggressive or destructive behaviors.

- Try to create situations in which the child can interact positively with his/her peers and not become overstimulated or frustrated–for example, sharing the carrying of an object or working together to sponge off a table.

- Remember, this child may need more adult supervision than is usual in order to interact positively in group situations.

- Because these children often receive so much negative feedback from adults and peers, the teacher should try to minimize negative comments or reactions as much as possible. Instead, state what the expected behavior is–for example: "You need to try to keep your feet on the floor" (child kicking underside of table).

- Observe and keep a record of the child during different activities, at different times of day, in different environments, and when he/she is alone with an adult or with peers. This will help teachers to determine the child's patterns of behavior and how different aspects of the environment influence his/her behavior.

7. can be rude and tactless.

8. may blame others for his/her problems.

SOCIAL/EMOTIONAL CONSEQUENCES

As a consequence of all of the above, children with ADD and/or ADHD often:

1. have poor self-esteem.

2. find it difficult to form and maintain friendships.

- Try to determine which activities seem to calm the child and what circumstances seem to overstimulate. In planning the curriculum, keep this knowledge in mind.

- Chart and record the child's behavior.

- Entries should be made at regular intervals, and the child's file should be reviewed and evaluated on a regular basis.

- Try to be calm and positive when dealing with the child.

- Work toward developing a trusting relationship with the parents that will enable staff and parents to share information about the child's behavior at home and at school.

Note: Many children with Attention Deficit/Hyperactive Disorder are put on drug therapy programs to tone down their behavior and improve the span of their attention. In these cases, it is especially important to share your observations with the parents and outside specialists.

Look for, observe, record, and share the following with other staff, professionals and parents:
- no change/or noticeable changes in behavior
- lethargic reactions
- drowsiness
- phasing out
- improved attending
- less impulsivity
- changes in eating habits
- specific times of the day when the child is more/less active.

Note: It is important for staff, parents, psychologists, and other professionals to share their observations and ideas and work together to develop a plan to meet the specific needs of the child.

RESOURCES

LOCAL

Children's mental health clinics

Services through local hospitals, boards of education, recreation organizations

Parent groups

Organizations for learning disabilities often have groups for children with ADHD and ADD

UNITED STATES

Attention Deficit Disorder
National Office
1788 Second Street, Suite 200
Highland Park, IL 60035
Tel: 1-847-432-2332
Online: http://www.add.org

CHADD
8181 Professional Place, Suite 201
Landover MD 20785
Tel: 1-800-233-4050
Online: http://www.chadd.org

The Council for Exceptional Children
1110 North Glebe Road, Suite 300
Arlington, VA 22201-5704
Tel: 1-888-232-7733
Online: http://www.cec.sped.org

CANADA

Canadian Council for Exceptional Children
Box 56012
Stoney Creek, Ontario L8G5C9
Tel: 1-204-452-1985
Online: http://www.canadian.cec.sped.org

CH.A.DD. Canada Inc.
Canada Children and Adults with Attention
    Deficit Disorders
National Office
1376 Bank Street
Ottawa, Ontario K1H 7Y3
Tel: 1-613-731-1209
Online: http://www.chaddcanada.org

Learning Disabilities Association of Canada
National Office
323 Chapel Street
Ottawa, Ontario K1N 7Z2
Tel: 1-613-238-5721
Online: http://www.ldac-taac.ca

Uniquely ADD/ADHD
368, 1440-52 Street NE
Calgary, Alberta T2A 4T8
Tel: 1-403-204-2393
Online: http://www.uniquely-adhd.com

ADDITIONAL RESOURCES

AUTISM SPECTRUM DISORDER
(Pervasive Developmental Disorders)

Autism Spectrum Disorder includes Autistic Disorder, Childhood Disintegrative Disorder, Rett Syndrome (Disorder), Asperger Syndrome (Disorder), and Pervasive Developmental Disorder Not Otherwise Specified.

An Autism Spectrum Disorder is basically a complex, severe pervasive developmental disorder that becomes evident before three years of age. It is a lifelong neurological problem that is marked by difficulties in social interaction, communication skills, ritualistic/compulsive behaviors, and in most instances impaired intellectual functioning is also evident. Autism Spectrum Disorder (with the exception of Rett's Disorder), is found more frequently in males. Not all stated symptoms are seen in all children, and the severity of a symptom may vary widely from child to child. Because symptoms vary so widely from one child to the next, there is no one single treatment/educational approach that works for all.

Common associated disorders include Intellectual Disabilities and Epileptic Seizures.

The cause or causes of Autism Spectrum Disorder are still unconfirmed. There appears, at this time, to be a strong genetic basis for autism. What is known is that autism is a brain disorder that affects the way the brain receives, processes, uses, and/or transmits information. It is not, as once popularly believed to be, the result of poor parenting.

Prognosis: If autism is diagnosed early, and intervention and treatment are started at an early age (depending on how severe the disorder is), the child may be able to overcome or lessen the impact of many of the symptoms, some of which potentially could lead to difficulties in coping in any and all parts of his/her future life.

AUTISTIC DISORDER

SOCIAL/EMOTIONAL ADAPTIVE BEHAVIORS	Alternative Considerations and Conditions	Recommendations
The child who has autism may 1. be unable to read social clues such as facial expressions, voice tone, nonverbal reactions—for example, frowning. 2. not respond when called by name (appears deaf). 3. lack social gestures, such as waving, smiling. 4. have little, inappropriate, or no eye contact; use a fixed or averted gaze. 5. respond inappropriately to situations—for example, laugh when scolded or hurt.	**Hearing Impairment** **Visual Impairment**	• Encourage games and activities that involve social interaction and physical touching. See **Attention Deficit Disorder, Learning Disabilities,** and **Intellectual Disabilities** for program ideas that may be useful. • If the child is staring off into space, use innovative techniques—noisy toys, actively moving objects, physical touch, or gestural sign language—to try to bring the child out of his/her withdrawal.

6. have very few play skills and leisure activities.

7. show excessive, seemingly unreasonable fears to new situations such as haircuts, fingernail clipping, new people, changes in the environment–for example, seeing an animal, taking a boat ride, and so on.

8. resist or be very upset by change in schedule, placement of furniture, and any other changes that influence the usual pattern in his/her daily living.

9. appear slow to relate and develop relationships with familiar adults and other children. Prefers isolated play.

10. not show normal anxiety toward strangers.

11. tend to be happy to spend time alone; does not seek others to share enjoyment.

12. lack imaginative play skills and have little appropriate interactions with other children.

13. exhibit a lot of random movement, such as wandering, or very little movement (stays in one place, focusing on a repetitive movement).

14. have immature and unusual emotional reactions and responses.

15. indicate little or no recognition of cause/effect relationships.

16. lack regular facial expressions, but will grimace for no obvious reason.

Behavioral/Social/Emotional Problems

Abuse/Neglect

Lack of previous opportunity to interact with other children

Failure to Thrive

Intellectual Disabilities

- Try to maintain eye contact while interacting with the child, but do not force it. The child often cannot listen and look at the same time. Avoid saying, "Look at me" when speaking to him/her.

- Use "hand over hand" to help him/her use new tools–for example, drawing.

- Ease the child into situations that are new or that may be scary for the child. It may be necessary to let the child bring a favorite toy or object along for extra security.

- Encourage the child to use "social" language–names of people, appropriate greetings when people enter or when someone leaves, and so on. If the child is nonverbal, he/she can shake hands.

- Model appropriate play behavior, starting out at his/her level. Children with Autism Spectrum Disorder often need to be taught (need to see in order to learn) how to play.

- Intercede quickly, using distraction; remove the child from the situation if aggressive action occurs.

- Keep the child from destroying other children's activities. The teacher may need to remove the child from the area–using distraction or redirection is often effective.

- Make sure that the toys he/she plays with are durable. Supply the child with appropriate things if he/she wants to rip, tear, or knock over.

17. wander off from the group and be unaware that he/she is lost.

18. not exhibit sympathy for or insight into other's feelings; appear cold and indifferent.

19. be aggressive and/or have destructive behaviors toward self and others.

20. have temper tantrums and scream and/or cry for no apparent reason–cannot be comforted when upset.

21. take objects that attract him/her such as food or objects that have a familiar appearance (look like something at home).

    Note: The child will probably have no sense of what does/does not belong to him/her. For this reason, that which may be seen as stealing is not perceived or understood this way by the child.

22. The child may allow peers to take things that belong to him/her because he/she has not developed a concept of ownership.

PHYSICAL/MOTOR BEHAVIORS

The child may

1. be unable to imitate other's actions or sounds.

2. exhibit ritualistic, repetitive movement: hand flapping, spinning of objects,

Behavioral/Social/Emotional Problems

Hearing Impairment
Visual Impairment

- In outdoor play, make sure that the child does not wander off. He/she most likely will have no concept of "getting lost."

- In a store environment, or where he/she is with objects that can be removed or broken, try to make sure that his/her hands are involved in carrying or pushing something.

- Use social stories (if the child comprehends language) to introduce new or unusual situations, or to guide the child through tasks or activities that have been difficult for him/her in the past.

Note: Children with an Autism Spectrum Disorder should wear a Medic Alert bracelet at all times.

- Do not overreact to ritualistic and withdrawal behaviors, but try to redirect the child to some new activity, or try to expand on his/her repetitive action, guiding the behavior into a more acceptable or social interaction.

- Try to involve the child in activities that will demand active participation, such as use of hands or other body movements. If possible, do not allow him/her to withdraw from interaction with others.

- Follow through on setting necessary limits, giving clear verbal and nonverbal messages. Staff may need to physically guide the child.

rocking rhythmically, dipping, body pos-turing, clapping, flicking, and so on.

3. respond unusually to sensory input–smell, touch, taste, sounds, and textures.

4. make loud repetitive sounds.

5. be a picky eater or eat nonedible sub-stances.

6. walk on toes or balls of his/her feet.

7. have unusual gross and/or fine motor coordination; have unusual gait; does not swing arms when walking, shuffles.

8. show little or no response or be overly dramatic in response to pain, hot or cold temperatures, or temperature changes.

9. have a preoccupation, for example, with light switches, flushing toilets, opening and closing doors.

10. be self-abusive: hitting, scratching, bit-ing, pulling out own hair, or banging self, at the same time not indicating any feeling of pain.

11. respond unusually to human touch–for example, may avoid cuddling (soft touching) but get enjoyment out of roughhousing (hard touching).

12. use toys/objects in repetitive, stereotypic ways, such as using one toy or type of toy, repeating one motion over and over.

13. be aggressive to others; be upset if he/she feels cornered with no way to escape.

Learning Disabilities (Sensory Integration Dysfunction)

Nutritional Deficiencies (pica*)
* pica is defined on p. 147

Cerebral Palsy

Abuse/Neglect

Behavioral/Social/Emotional Problems

Learning Disabilities (Sensory Integration Dysfunction)

Behavioral/Social/Emotional Problems

- If a child is self-abusive, gently hold his/her hands, and/or cradle his/her body, and say "no." Singing and rocking back and forth often calms the child and stops the self-abusive actions.

- Because the child may not respond to pain or discomfort, staff need to monitor him/her for possible injuries or illnesses.

- Make sure the child is dressed appropri-ately for the weather. The child may refuse to do this because he/she may not respond to hot or cold and/or may not like the feel/texture of the clothing.

- Because this child may eat any substances in the environment, it is especially impor-tant to remove all poisonous materials that are not edible from the environment–including outdoor or indoor plants, and other things one might not necessarily remove from an average classroom.

- Encourage games and activities that involve social interaction and physical touching.

- Teach specific skills such as bike riding. Staff may need to physically put him/her through the motions of how to do it.

- Some children will fixate on certain objects, colors, or repetitive movements (perseveration-withdrawal behavior). Try to find ways to break this pattern without creating a big issue over it–for example, distracting, placing object where child can see it and knows where it is; setting up room without the toy that creates the perseverative (withdrawal-type) behavior, and so on.

14. often be healthy and physically attractive in appearance.

15. have epileptic seizures (**Note:** this is more common in adolescence).

16. have perceptual/spatial problems—for example, spatial but not depth perception, therefore may climb to dangerous heights.

17. be hyperactive or hypoactive.

18. have frequent tantrums; sudden outbursts of anger (the cause cannot always be determined).

19. be unaware of dangers, such as cars and heights.

20. have sleep problems.

21. have allergies and/or food intolerance.

COMMUNICATION CHARACTERISTICS (Speech and Language)

The child may

1. not have babbled as an infant.

2. lack nonverbal communication skills such as nodding, gesturing, pointing, or appropriate facial expressions.

3. have little or no language or had some language development and then regressed to no language.

4. use more nonverbal than verbal language—for example, pulling a person to a place to get a desired object.

Attention Deficit/Hyperactive Disorder Learning Disabilities

Hearing Impairment

Note: Some children with Autism Spectrum Disorder may at times be extremely disruptive and have behaviors that are difficult to manage. Avoid using a toy that creates repetitive, withdrawal behavior, or putting the child into isolation—which then allows the child to withdraw into him-/herself. It is important to give the child a safe space and time to calm down, and then to help him/her to become involved in a positive and interactive play situation.

- Allow the child to take the teacher by the hand and get his/her needs met. The teacher should use language to express what that need was—for example, "You want juice."

- Give clear, concise statements when talking.

- Accompany verbal statements with physical actions and nonverbal gestures ("Come here"—take the child's hand, point to the area you wish to go to, or guide the child in that direction).

- It may be necessary to show the child how to do something by physically guiding him/her through the desired action—for example, taking his/her hand with crayon in it and using a "hand over hand" motion to guide the child's hand in drawing around an object that he/she wants to trace.

- Encourage social language (verbal and nonverbal greetings).

- Sing directions to the child.

5. lack emotional tone, even when crying.

6. use vocal sounds—grunting, bellowing, and so on.

7. not respond to verbal communication (appears deaf).

8. echo words that others have said, immediately, or from something heard previously (immediate echolalia versus delayed echolalia).

9. sing before he/she speaks.

10. have stereotyped, repetitive use of words and/or phrases.

11. have immature grammatical structure.

12. confuse personal pronouns—you, mine, yours, and so on.

13. repeat jingles or television commercials word for word.

14. have unusual articulation, speech sounds, voice sounds, and fluency.

15. have problems with speech and language that make it difficult for the listener to understand.

16. lack functional social language (as used in social greetings and in initiating and maintaining conversation).

17. indulge in lengthy monologues on his/her favorite topics, regardless of interjections from the listeners. There is no expectation that the listener might make comments or ask questions.

Tourette Syndrome (Disorder)

Elective/Selective Mutism

Cultural Influences/English as a Second Language/English with a Dialect

Speech and Language Problems

Learning Disabilities

- Use pictures to increase vocabulary and to tell stories.

- Picture Lotto (game where picture of object/animal is matched with same object/animal or associated object/animal on a playing board) will help with matching skills and vocabulary.

- See **Speech and Language Problems** for ideas.

- Model correct English pronoun usage.

- Tell and act out social stories to help the child experience appropriate interaction in social situations.

- If the child tends to focus on one topic, encourage expansion of his/her ideas and add new ideas.

- Expect only short periods of focused learning. Reward periods of focused learning with things the child enjoys, such as music or a favorite book or toy, or rocking chair.

See **Cerebral Palsy (Augmentative Communication Systems)**.

For additional ideas, see recommendations under:
Learning Disabilities
Intellectual Disabilities
Motor Problems
Learning Disabilities/Sensory Integration Dysfunction
Speech and Language Problems
Attention Deficit/Hyperactive Disorder
Allergies (Food Intolerance)
Epilepsy

18. have difficulty understanding or comprehending the spoken word, answering questions, following directions, and/or making verbal choices.

19. be easily frustrated because of his/her lack of understanding of the world around him/her and because of this child's inability to communicate clearly his/her wants and needs.

PRE-ACADEMIC/ACADEMIC LEARNING STYLES

The child may

1. have uneven development of cognitive skills–high functioning in some areas, low in others. He/she may also have mild to severe learning disabilities.

   Note: Remember, autism is a brain disorder that affects the way the brain receives, processes, and transmits information.

2. have or not have good visual/spatial skills.

3. have good rote memory for visual/spatial material.

4. not be able to imitate what the adult has shown him/her to do.

5. have special skills in arithmetic.

6. have special skills in music and/or art.

7. pursue one aspect of learning to the exclusion of other areas or topics.

Learning Disabilities

8. repeat the same question or topic many times.

9. have poor attention span for topics in which he/she is not interested and excellent attention for preferred topics.

10. read but not comprehend what he/she has read.

11. express him-/herself well on favorite topics.

12. have difficulty with transition times.

13. be a better visual and tactile learner than an auditory learner.

ASPERGER SYNDROME (DISORDER)

Children with **Asperger Syndrome (Disorder)** display many of the same behavioral characteristics as children with autism.

PHYSICAL AND BEHAVIORAL CHARACTERISTICS

The major differences are that children who have Asperger Syndrome (Disorder) have

1. no significant intellectual delays.

2. age-appropriate language skills, self-help skills, and adaptive behaviors (excluding social development).

   Note: Asperger Syndrome (Disorder) is often not diagnosed until later (six years of age). Like autism it is more prevalent in boys than in girls.

Attention Deficit/Hyperactive Disorder

Cultural Influences/English as a Second Language/English with a Dialect

Note: A child who has been very deprived or abused may respond out of emotional stress in ways that appear autistic. Look for improvement (change) in the child's behavior as he/she settles into the program.
Learning Disabilities

Note: Be aware that the "subboxes" are not definitions as they are incomplete without the characteristics listed below.

Learning Disabilities

- Show appreciation of the child's intellectual ability, encouraging further learning and creative expansion of interests into art projects that may demand working with paint and glue (which the child may have tended to avoid).

- It is important to find situations in which the child needs to interact with peers in a positive manner. The child with Asperger's

Syndrome (Disorder) may need a great deal of support in finding ways in which to interact positively with his/her peers.

- Because the child with Asperger Syndrome (Disorder) is intellectually capable, one should be able to use reasoning as a means of helping him/her to learn interaction skills. (For example, "To be safe crossing the street we need to hold hands with a partner to make sure both the partner and you are safe and watching out for each other.")

RETT SYNDROME (DISORDER)

Children with **Rett Syndrome (Disorder)** display many of the same behavioral characteristics as those with autism.

The major difference is that these children have apparent normal development in the early months, followed by

1. loss of previously acquired verbal language and social interaction skills.
2. decreased rate of head growth.
3. the development of stereotypical hand movements (losing purposeful movement).
4. a gait that is usually wide based and stiff legged.
5. autistic-like behaviors.

Note: Rett Syndrome (Disorder) is much more common in girls than in boys. Because overall deterioration continues, the prognosis for the future is not positive.

Behavioral/Social/Emotional Problems

- See recommendations listed under **Autism**.

Curvature of the Spine
Muscular Dystrophy

CHILDHOOD DISINTEGRATIVE DISORDER

> Children with **Childhood Disintegrative Disorder** display many of the same behavioral characteristics as children with autism.

The major differences are that these children have seemingly normal development in all areas of development up to the age of 2 years, and at times longer, though no longer than 10 years of age, followed by

1. loss of many of the skills previously acquired–for example, motor, language, social skills, and adaptive behaviors.

2. development of abnormal functioning in two or more of these areas.

   Note: Childhood Disintegrative Disorder is most commonly found in boys.

PERVASIVE DEVELOPMENTAL DISORDER NOT OTHERWISE SPECIFIED

> **Pervasive Developmental Disorder** is a term used when a child has severe pervasive impairments in all developmental areas: motor, language, social, and adaptive skills, but whose symptoms do not exactly fit within the parameters for other Autism Spectrum Disorders. It may also be referred to as "Atypical Autism."

Learning Disabilities

Visual Impairment
Hearing Impairment

RESOURCES

LOCAL

Associations, organizations, and societies for children with autism and their parents

Services through university clinics and hospital out-service clinics

Boards of Education

UNITED STATES

Asperger's Syndrome Coalition of the United States, Inc.
P.O. Box 49267
Jacksonville, FL 32240-9267
Tel: 1-904-745-6741
Online: http://www.asperger.org

Asperger's Syndrome Education Network
Tel: 1-732-321-0880
Online: http://www.aspennj.org

Autism Network International
P.O. Box 35448
Syracuse, NY 13235-5448
Online: http://ani.autistics.org

Autism Society of America
7910 Woodmount Avenue, Suite 300
Bethesda, MD 20814-3067
Tel: 1-800-328-8476
Online: http://www.autism-society.org

Exploring Autism
Box 3445 DUMC
Durham, NC 27710
Online: www.exploringautism.org
    (Asperger Syndrome [Disorder], Childhood Disintegrative Disorder, Pervasive Developmental Disorder, Rett Syndrome [Disorder])

International Rett Syndrome Association
9121 Piscataway Road, Suite 2B
Clinton, MD 20735
Tel: 1-800-818-7388
Online: http://www.rettsyndrome.org

CANADA

Asperger's Society of Ontario
293 Wychwood Avenue
Toronto, Ontario M6C 2T6
Tel: 1-416-651-4037
Online: http://www.aspergersyndrome.ca

Autism Society of Canada
1179 King Street West, Suite 004
Toronto, Ontario M6K 3C5
Tel: 1-416-246-9592
Online: http://www.autismsociety.on.ca

Autism Treatment Services of Canada
404-94th Avenue SE
Calgary, Alberta T2J 0E8
Tel: 1-403-253-6961
Online: http://www.autism.ca

Geneva Centre for Autism
250 Davisville Avenue, Suite 200
Toronto, Ontario M4S 1H2
Tel: 1-416-322-7877
Online: http://www.autism.net

Ontario Rett Syndrome Association
P.O. Box 75014
Bolton, Ontario L7E 1H6
Tel: 1-519-850-7388
Online: http://www.rettsyndrome.on.ca

Rett Syndrome Research Foundation
4600 Devitt Drive
Cincinnati, OH 45246
Tel: 513-874-3020
Online: http://www.rsrf.org

ADDITIONAL RESOURCES

BEHAVIORAL/SOCIAL/EMOTIONAL PROBLEMS

Behavioral/Social/Emotional Problems may be considered/identified by the amount and intensity of the child's reactions when compared to other children of the same chronological age.

If a child exhibits too much or too little of a behavior or emotion, he/she may be seen as having a behavioral problem. It may also be considered a problem if a child exhibits a behavior that is inappropriate to a setting.

Behavioral problems are often found in conjunction with other exceptionalities, such as intellectual or physical disabilities. These may limit the areas in which the child is able to participate and cause frustration that in turn may result in a behavioral reaction or problem.

Note: It is only when inappropriate behavior continues over a long period of time, occurs frequently, is of considerable intensity, and requires specialized help that it is regarded as a behavioral/ social/emotional problem.

ACTING OUT

PHYSICAL AND BEHAVIORAL CHARACTERISTICS	Alternative Considerations and Conditions	Recommendations
The child may 1. be disruptive, impulsive, disorganized, and/or distractible. 2. be restless, irritable, anxious, have temper tantrums (explosive behavior). 3. have a short attention span, be unable to finish a task, have poor concentration. 4. be manipulative, be compulsive, bother others, be uncooperative in group situations. 5. require constant adult supervision. 6. be whiny and frequently cry. 7. make negative comments about him-/herself—for example, "I'm stupid," "I'm a coo-coo head." 8. talk excessively.	**Visual Impairment** **Hearing Impairment** **Intellectual Disabilities** **Cultural Influences/English as a Second Language/English with a Dialect** Little or no previous social experience **Attention Deficit/Hyperactive Disorder (ADHD)** Difficult home environment Modeling in the home	• Chart the child's behavior—incident, time of day, actual behavior, and situations that may have triggered specific behaviors. • Contact the parents to discuss the child's behavior at home. • Goals should be to involve the child in positive social experiences and to be as encouraging and positive as often as possible. • Ignore the negative behavior and try to reinforce those things that the child does that are positive. • Explain the rules and routines carefully so that the child knows what is expected. If possible, try to let the child know each day what the program plan is, thus easing any fears he/she has of the unexpected. Using a pictorial format for mapping out the day's plan may be very helpful to children who do not easily comprehend verbal messages or have transition problems.

9. be unable to relax.

10. display attention-getting behaviors.

11. have emotional shifts or rigidity (unable to adapt to change).

12. display hyperactivity.

WITHDRAWN

The child may

1. be fearful, avoid eye contact, cry easily.

2. be quiet, be clinging, be shy.

3. show no affection, be expressionless, have sluggish actions.

4. demonstrate consistent thumbsucking, masturbation, hair twirling, nail biting, perseveration (repetitive actions).

5. not interact with peers; play alone.

6. lack self-confidence (withdraws from trying).

7. have excessive fears or anxieties.

8. have an inability to learn.

9. always be tired.

10. be able to express ideas and use words effectively, but is selective as to where and to whom he/she will talk (see **Elective/Selective Mutism**, p. 44).

Different expectations between home and school

The child may be extremely shy by temperament.
Autism Spectrum Disorder
Abuse/Neglect

Cultural Influences/English as a Second Language/English with a Dialect

Autism Spectrum Disorder

The child may have had little previous experience in playing with other children or in being away from home.

Intellectual Disabilities

Nonverbal **(Speech and Language Problems)**

- Some children will "act out" until the adult places limits. This is often a cry for help. Try to anticipate when a child is beginning to lose control and move in before the behavior becomes extreme. Try to help him/her find positive alternatives to deal with the situation that is causing the behavior.

- A supportive hand on the shoulder may help a child to relax and to avoid losing control.

- Aggressive feelings can be released through the use of punching bags, play dough, and clay.

- Puppets and dress-up activities also provide outlets for emotions.

- Water, sand play, finger painting, and other messy activities often relax a tense child.

- A quiet corner where a child can play quietly provides an alternative environment for a child who needs time to calm down and refocus.

- Regardless of what the problem is, it is important to

 –accept the child and try to build trust.

 –reduce, if possible eliminate, opportunities for failure.

 –individualize instruction so that the child can succeed.

 –be understanding, but set firm limits on behavior.

 –give choices wherever possible (this empowers the child).

EXTREME BEHAVIORAL CHARACTERISTICS

Extreme behaviors can include any and all of the above indicated behaviors, as well as

1. self-mutilating (hurting actions).

2. actions that intentionally hurt others.

3. withdrawal into self; little or no relationship with others.

4. total loss of self-control and an inability to retain control (breaks objects, throws objects, hits objects, or flings self against objects or people). The child may have a complete break with reality at times. Staff will be unable to reach him/her no matter how hard they try; yet at other times his/her behavior appears normal.

5. very low threshold for frustration or stress. The child may lose self-control with only slight provocation.

6. talking to him-/herself; the child may believe that he/she is some animal or imaginary character—and cannot be pulled out of it.

7. having extreme fears and losing self-control easily.

8. having no sense of danger.

9. being cruel to people and/or animals.

10. exhibiting inappropriate sexual behavior for his/her age.

11. not be able to differentiate between truth and lying—always putting the blame on the other person.

Autism Spectrum Disorder

Abuse/Neglect

–provide stability, be fair, firm, and consistent.

–provide opportunities for decision making and independent activities that allow the child to become more mature.

–encourage the peer group to accept and support the child.

–give praise for work well done.

–teach relaxation, such as yoga, music, breathing exercises. Using a rocking chair will also relax a child.

–use stories and dramatic play to teach the child how to express negative and positive feelings. Use something like puppets or "Me and My Friends" kit.

Note: If a child exhibits continuously inappropriate behavior to an abnormal degree, and if he/she displays deviant and delayed development in other basic functions such as language and motor skills, it is important that the center recommend that the child be referred for a developmental assessment. Specialized programming is imperative.

Note: If the parents do not follow up on recommendations for referral, teachers should make sure that a consultant to the center, or a local child welfare agency worker, assists teachers in developing an action plan for the child in the setting, while encouraging the parents to obtain an assessment and, if necessary, specialized help.

OPPOSITIONAL DEFIANT DISORDER (O.D.D.)

Oppositional Defiant Disorder is a condition that is characterized by consistent negative and defiant behavior. Typically, the child will repeatedly act disobediently, be hostile, stubborn, and resistant to suggestions.

Anger and hostility may be focused on peers and/or adults.

Children who have Oppositional Defiant Disorder often also have Attention Deficit Hyperactive Disorder and/or depression and/or anxiety.

PHYSICAL AND BEHAVIORAL CHARACTERISTICS

Typical behaviors include

1. frequent loss of temper.
2. being argumentative with adults and/or peers.
3. being stubborn, unwilling to compromise.
4. doing things that annoy others.
5. becoming easily annoyed by others.
6. blaming others for things that he/she has done.
7. frequently ignoring limits and rules.
8. being resentful and resistant.
9. being spiteful and/or vindictive.

Important Questions to Ask

1. In what ways is O.D.D. evident in this child's behavior? (Describe)
2. At what age was the behavior first noticed?
3. What organization/professional diagnosed Oppositional Defiant Disorder? With whom is the family currently working?
4. How is the child's behavior handled at home?
5. What previous experience has the child had in interacting with peers? How did he/she manage in this situation?
6. Is the child on any medication? If yes, for how long? Will the staff need to administer medication while the child is present at the center?

Recommendations

- It is extremely important that there be on-going communication between the home, the center, and any professional organization that is working with the child. A daily communication book that goes between home and center is extremely important.

- This child needs firm, consistent, and positive limits. It is particularly important to immediately respond to any positive behavior because this child probably has received a great deal of negative reaction due to his/her angry or hostile behavior.

- Try to find ways that calm the child and use these as frequently as possible. Once the child is calm and able to talk, try to help him/her to figure out some new ways of interacting and/or responding to adults and peers.

43

- If the child becomes easily overstimulated, help the child to find ways to remove self from situation, seek adult support, find a calming space, and so on.

- Work consistently to help the child to develop self-discipline techniques. For example, when the child is angry and about to hit someone, teach the child to put his/her hands in pockets or behind the back, and/or to focus on his/her hands while saying to him/her, "Hands do not hit."

- Try to set short- and long-term goals with the child in order to help him/her control difficult behaviors.

- Help the child to learn how to talk about his/her feelings; to be able to admit when he/she has done something inappropriate. This means that the adult has to be accepting, supportive, and able to give positive suggestions.

- Positive, physical outlets for energy are usually important for this child.

- Use "social stories," videos, puppets, and other resources to teach appropriate behaviors.

ELECTIVE/SELECTIVE MUTISM

Elective/Selective Mutism is a somewhat rare childhood condition in which the child who is able to talk does not talk to certain people or in certain places. It is believed that this condition is triggered by anxiety and fear of unknown responses from certain people or in certain places (e.g., school; a child care center; visiting people outside of the family).

The prognosis for mutism is very positive. Sometimes it just slowly disappears on its own; sometimes it disappears suddenly—the child is not talking one day and the next day begins to talk actively.

It is best not to make a big thing of it, but to act as if the child is talking, responding to any nonverbal indications, including the child in activities, and so on. In a school or group situation, sometimes a child will begin to whisper softly. People should respond to any attempts the child makes to communicate verbally. Try to follow through with actions that positively reinforce the child's verbal communication.

Note: Sometimes it helps to tape record the child in a place where he/she talks/sings freely, such as the home setting, and then ask him/her to bring the tape to a place where he/she is selectively mute and share it. This can also "break the ice" for the child.

RESOURCES

LOCAL

Mental health associations/clinics

Preschool and school programs for children with behavioral problems/disorders

Hospital out-patient services

Different areas have different agencies that sponsor programs to support families who have children with behavioral/social/emotional problems

UNITED STATES

Council for Children with Behavioral Disorders
Council for Exceptional Children
Two Ballston Plaza
1110 N Glebe Road
Arlington, VA 22201
Online: http://www.ccbd.net

National Institutes of Mental Health
6001 Executive Boulevard
Room 8184, MSC 9663
Bethesda, MD 20892-9663
Tel: 1-301-443-4513
Online: http://www.nimh.nih.gov

Mental Health Matters
Online: http://www.mental-health-matters.com

National Mental Health Association
2001 N. Beauregard Street, 12th Floor
Alexandria, VA 22311
Tel: 1-703-684-7722

Mental Health Resource Center
Tel: 1-800-969-6642
Online: http://www.nmha.org

United States Department of Health and Human
   Services
The Center for Mental Health Sciences
P.O. Box 42490
Washington, D.C. 20015
Tel: 1-800-789-2647
Online: http://www.mentalhealth.org

CANADA

Canadian Mental Health Association
National Office
2160 Yonge Street, 3rd Floor
Toronto, Ontario M4S 2Z3
Tel: 1-416-484-7750
Online: http://www.cmha.ca

CEREBRAL PALSY

Cerebral Palsy is a condition characterized by involuntary abnormalities of movement of the muscles of the arms, legs, face, and neck.

This condition is usually caused by a lack of oxygen to the brain, resulting in permanent but nonprogressive damage to the motor center of the brain. There are also other causes of brain damage, such as car accidents that result in conditions resembling cerebral palsy. The damage usually occurs during the pregnancy, immediately before birth, or during birth. Not all the symptoms may be evident until the child is about 18 months of age, after which time this condition is nonprogressive. At times there may also be problems in speech, swallowing, vision, hearing, and/or perception. Constipation, respiratory infections, and seizures may also be more prevalent in children with cerebral palsy.

The movement disorders of this condition are not usually evident during sleep.

PHYSICAL AND BEHAVIORAL CHARACTERISTICS	Essential Information	Recommendations
1. There is a tremendous range of disability –from minimal to severe coordination problems; from no delay to severe delay in intellectual functioning. 2. Many children who have Cerebral Palsy may seem more intellectually delayed than they actually are. Poor coordination and poor control of muscles needed for speech may affect the clarity of speech. 3. Physical coordination/involuntary movement problems may be in one or more of the limbs; may be involved in one side of the body only; and may or may not impede the activity level of the child.	Find out what type of therapy or medical attention the child is receiving. Speak with the therapist to find out ways in which staff might be able to support the therapeutic goals. If the child is in a wheelchair, wears braces, or uses other devices, staff must know how to adjust and fold the chair, set up and/or be able to remove the child from a device, and support the child in whatever else is necessary. To ensure that inclusion will be a positive experience: 1. Make sure that the teachers and other people working with the child on a daily basis understand the condition and have a positive attitude about inclusion.	• Make sure that the center keeps in contact with any agency working with this child. • The basic goal is to find ways in which this child can be included in all aspects of the program. • Give the child as many life experiences as possible, such as handling animals and taking trips. • See **Sensory Integration Dysfunction Recommendations** (under **Learning Disabilities**). • Work with all different media (playdough, clay, sand, water, fingerpaint, and so on), even though it may be difficult if the child is in braces or a wheelchair. This type of experience is important and can support the development of fine motor skills.

At times, Cerebral Palsy will go undiagnosed:

In infants, if cerebral palsy is suspected, look for

1. tense posture.

2. retracted head (thrust back).

3. tight-fisting of hands.

4. extension and tension in legs.

5. these characteristics often may be accompanied by irritable behavior.

In older children, look for

1. poor gross motor skills.

2. poor fine motor skills, tension or trembling in fingers and/or hands.

3. some slurring of speech.

2. Be sure to check out ahead of time whether this child is in braces or a wheelchair; make sure that the center is physically able to meet his/her needs (breadth of doorways and size/shape of classrooms, number of stairs, accessibility of outdoor play), and so on.

3. Be sure staff can accommodate this child's needs—lifting, carrying upstairs and downstairs in emergencies, and providing supervision during outdoor play.

If Cerebral Palsy is suspected in an infant or older child who has a coordination problem that has not been diagnosed, suggest to the parents that they have a pediatrician do a developmental examination.

- Children with Cerebral Palsy may have had little previous opportunity for playing with other children; therefore, teachers may have to develop activities that foster playing together, and that will support learning to share and take turns such as
  —doll center opportunities
  —using and interacting with puppets
  —dress-up clothes.

- Teachers may need to encourage use of hands—grasping, balancing, and manipulating small toys and materials such as
  —small blocks
  —large peg boards
  —large Lego-type fitting together games
  —busy boxes
  —clay, playdough, plasticine
  —fingerpaint, and so on.

- Think in terms of seating arrangements that enable the child to be as much a part of the group as possible. Special seats are now available that give support and are designed to meet the individual needs of the child.

- In outdoor activity time, find ways in which the child can participate with his/her peers so that they will not feel left out. This may mean finding a specialist who can design (with the approval and support of the child's doctor) special harnesses and trike-type toys so that the child can participate as fully as possible with his/her peers.

AUGMENTATIVE COMMUNICATION SYSTEMS

Augmentative Communication is the use of alternative methods of communicating that do not rely on vocal expression or fine motor skills of the hands and fingers.

Alternative methods to speech include using

- real objects to try to get the meaning across or to clarify the meaning of a word, or for enabling a child to make a choice.
- natural gestures such as body orientation, pointing, touching, gazing, and signing gestures.
- personal photograph boards (actual photos of the child). For example, the child wants to go in the car. He/she then can go over and choose the picture of him-/herself riding in the car.
- picture boards–the child indicates, by pointing to a picture, what it is he/she wants.
- communication boards (such as "Bliss Symbols")
- picture or object (real or copy of) exchange. The child gets his/her needs/wants met by choosing a picture/object and taking it to an adult to get the real thing he/she wants or needs–for example, the child brings a picture of an apple to the staff in order to get a real apple (PECS–Picture Exchange Communication System).
- written words (which child learns and can than use to communicate).
- computers (keys specially indented to steady fingers).
- physical aids, such as a pointer worn on a headband or a specially molded pillow that supports and increases arm control.
- electronic devices, such as computer controlled communication devices.
- printed words with or without pictures.
- pictorial timetables to communicate what is going to happen–for example, timetable of expectations and activities during the day; or of what the child is supposed to do (a sequenced task).

Choosing an alternative to speech necessitates finding a method that is compatible to the range of levels in different areas of development, as well as the specific needs of the user. The following must be taken into consideration.

The child's
- linguistic ability–for example, speaks very little or not easily understood
- cognitive development–for example, average, below average, or has learning disabilities
- sensory input–for example, is visually and/or hearing impaired
- physical development–for example, motor control of mouth, vocal organs, and/or hands and fingers
- social development–for example, does not relate to parents, teachers, and/or peers; beginning to show signs of wanting to engage others in order to express his/her wants/needs; tries to participate, for example, in play with adults/peers; seeks help from others.

Questions to Consider

1. Will staff, family, peers, and others be able to use and understand the system without extensive training?

2. Is the system portable? Can it be used in a range of different situations? Is it a system that does not require elaborate or cumbersome equipment?

3. Is the system usable? Does the system enable the individual to communicate with those who are currently involved with the child?

4. Does the system encourage inclusion in the school and community?

5. Does the system consist of a step toward the development of the ability to use speech?

Children with other types of special need who may benefit from the use of Augmentative Communication Systems may include those who have

- Autism Spectrum Disorder.
- Attention Deficit Disorder.
- Fetal Alcohol Syndrome.
- Fragile X Syndrome.
- Hearing Impairment.
- Intellectual Disabilities.
- Lead Poisoning.
- Muscular Dystrophy.
- Prematurity/ Preterm.
- Spina Bifida.
- Speech and Language Problems.
- Visual Impairment.

RESOURCES

LOCAL

Cerebral Palsy associations, societies, and Federations

Easter Seal Society

Physiotherapy services at local hospitals

Orthopedic clinics and specialists

UNITED STATES

March of Dimes
1275 Mamaroneck Avenue
White Plains, NY 10605
Online: http://www.modimes.org

National Ataxia Foundation (NAF)
2600 Fernbrook Lane, Suite 119
Minneapolis, MN 55447
Tel: 1-763-553-0020
Online: http://www.ataxia.org

CANADA

Easter Seals/March of Dimes
National Council
90 Eglinton Avenue East, Suite 511
Toronto, Ontario M4P 2Y3
Tel: 1-416-932-8382
Online: http://www.esmodnc.org

Speech pathologists

Speech clinics

Services available from education institutions or through university clinics

United Cerebral Palsy Association Inc. (UCP)
1660 L Street NW, Suite 700
Washington, DC 20036-5602
Tel: 1-800-872-5827
Online: http://www.ucpa.org

Ontario Federation for Cerebral Palsy
104-1630 Lawrence Avenue West
Toronto, Ontario M6L1C5
Tel: 1-877-244-9686
Online: http://www.ofcp.on.ca

ADDITIONAL RESOURCES

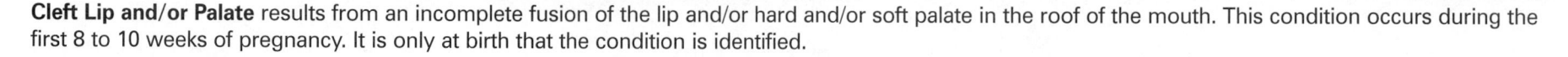

CLEFT LIP AND/OR PALATE

Cleft Lip and/or Palate results from an incomplete fusion of the lip and/or hard and/or soft palate in the roof of the mouth. This condition occurs during the first 8 to 10 weeks of pregnancy. It is only at birth that the condition is identified.

Many cleft lip and/or palates are genetic in origin. However, women who smoke, drink alcohol, or take high levels of vitamin A and/or are not taking an adequate amount of folic acid prior to pregnancy are at a higher risk for having a child with a cleft condition. It is recommended that about two months prior to pregnancy, women should take foods and vitamins with folic acid, a recognized preventative to cleft lip and/or palate formation.

SPECIFIC CONSIDERATIONS	Essential Information	Recommendations
Children with this condition may have some special needs in one or more of the following areas: **1. Food Intake** • Because of imperfect closure of the lips, sucking is often difficult for these children. If the hard and/or soft palates are also involved, food can become trapped in the upper part of the mouth or may leak out of the nose. It is important for the teacher of young children to be aware of any special needs in this area. To facilitate the intake of liquids, a special nipple for babies with this condition is available. • A plate may be fitted into the roof of the child's mouth in the months prior to the final surgery for a cleft palate. This will facilitate feeding. **2. Health** • Susceptibility to severe or persistent middle ear infections is common.	Corrective surgery is usually done in stages with these children. The initial surgery often occurs early in life, alleviating some of the food intake problems. The first operations for cleft lip can usually be done immediately after birth. Plastic surgery usually follows a few months later. Plastic surgery for cleft lip usually produces excellent results. The initial operation for cleft palate is often not done until 6 to 12 months of age. If this operation is delayed too long, permanent speech damage (nasal quality) may occur. Permission to contact the child's physician for information is imperative.	• It is important that this child be treated as normally as possible. He/she should be helped to become an active and accepted part of the group. • If children comment on the child's appearance, it is important to explain that each of us looks and acts differently. Some people run faster than others, some people are better than others at putting a puzzle together, and some people speak more clearly than others. It is perhaps most important to focus mainly on the common similarities of people, such as we all have two eyes, one nose, one mouth, and two arms. • If the subject of appearance is never brought up by the children and does not seem to be isolating the child in any way, it is not necessary for the teacher to feel compelled to discuss it. • Find out who the speech therapist is and whether there are any support activities that can be included in the school curriculum.

- It is important to know what the center is expected to do in the way of preventing infections, as well as whether an infection is suspected.

3. Teeth

- Teeth/mouth plates are frequently prescribed. The center needs to know any specific requirements concerning this equipment.

4. Speech

- Speech development is usually more difficult for children with this condition. Assessment is usually made by a speech pathologist, and the child often receives an individualized speech therapy program to be followed on a daily basis in home and school.

5. Voice Quality

- As a consequence of palate malformation, voice sounds are often nasal; pitch may be too low, loud, or high. A speech therapist can often help a child to modulate his/her quality of vocal tone.

6. Hospitalization

- Because of the need for repeated surgery to repair the lip and/or palate, or dental surgery to replace teeth, the child with a cleft lip and/or palate may have already experienced–and may be presently experiencing– periods of hospitalization. The center should be aware of special emotional and social needs that might result from this.

Be sure parents let center staff know ahead of time if the child is scheduled for special dental procedures or for additional surgery. This will enable the center to take this knowledge into consideration if the child should need additional emotional support at this time.

Speech and Language Problems

Behavioral/Social/Emotional Problems

- Do not isolate the child for special sessions of speech therapy in the school environment.

- If no specialist is involved, make sure all staff have professional guidance in working with this child.

- The child should be given opportunities to discuss feelings, hospital experiences, and other concerns. Do not pressure the child to share these feelings with the whole group unless the child initiates interest in doing this.

- Set up play areas like a doctor's office or hospital corner that will enable the child to play out his/her anxieties and experiences.

RESOURCES

LOCAL

Cleft lip/palate associations and parent support groups

Family service associations

Hospital/clinic dentistry specialists

Speech/Language clinics and hospitals

UNITED STATES

American Cleft Palate-Craniofacial Association
Cleft Palate Foundation
104 South Estes Drive, Suite 204
Chapel Hill, NC 27514
Tel: 1-800-242-5338
Online: http://www.cleftline.org

Cleft Lip and Palate Resource
Wide Smiles
P.O. Box 5153
Stockton, CA 95205-0153
Tel: 1-209-942-2812
Online: http://www.widesmiles.org

Cleft Advocate
Online: http://www.cleftadvocate.org

CANADA

Canadian Association of Oral and Maxillofacial
  Surgeons
174 Colonnade Road, Unit 26
Ottawa, Ontario K2E 7J5
Tel: 1-888-369-5641
Online: http://www.caoms.com

ADDITIONAL RESOURCES

CULTURAL INFLUENCES ON BEHAVIOR as well as ENGLISH AS A SECOND LANGUAGE/ENGLISH WITH A DIALECT

When we look at **Cultural Influences on Behavior** a number of variables have to be taken into consideration.

- The length of time a family has been settled in the new environment
- The amount of trauma (e.g., refugee camps) that a family has gone through in the course of immigrating
- Whether or not the parents understand and/or speak English
- Whether or not the child understands and/or speaks English
- Whether the child has been living with his/her parents or recently joined his/her parents after having been raised by grandparents, other relatives, or other persons in his/her home country
- The child's previous schooling—whether or not the child attended school on a regular basis
- The degree of stress and strain the family is presently experiencing due to financial needs, crowded living quarters, and/or problems in adjusting to the new environment, including weather conditions to which they are unaccustomed
- Male/female role differences between this country and the country of origin
- Food, housing, medical practices, customs, religious practices, special holidays/traditions, and so on, all of which can impact on behavior

It should be noted that reactions vary tremendously from child to child and from culture to culture. Some children will enter a new program and be fully adapted in a very short period of time; others may have considerable difficulty adjusting to the new setting.

PHYSICAL CONDITIONS	Alternative Considerations and Conditions	Recommendations
The child may 1. be frequently sick, especially with upper respiratory infections. 2. have sudden weight loss. 3. appear to tire easily. 4. appear withdrawn or depressed. 5. have blue marks on back and buttocks. This pigmentation is common in Asian preschoolers. It is called "Mongolian Spots." The blue color will remain even in color instead of fading as it would in a bruise. It will not be sore or puffy.	Medical problems not related to cultural influences include: **Asthma** Tonsil and adenoid infection **Cystic Fibrosis** **Diabetes** **Nutritional Deficiencies** **Abuse/Neglect** **Leukemia** **Abuse/Neglect** **Allergies** and **Food Intolerance**	• Try to avoid situations in which the child becomes chilled, wet, or overly exposed to extreme temperatures. • Encourage a medical checkup and follow up on any recommendations given by the physician. • Allow the child ample time to rest or retreat from others. (The home situation may be overly crowded, noisy, or very quiet.) • Do not try to force the child to interact or pay attention when he/she is not feeling well.

6. have scratch marks on the neck. This is commonly found in children from Vietnam, as well as from other Southeast Asian countries. This is a custom called "scratching the wind." When a child is sick, the parents scratch the shoulder blades of the child with a sharp spoon, believing that this will "let out the bad winds" and make the child well again.

7. sometimes have burns or several crescent shaped burns around the shoulders. Again, this is to draw out the poisonous winds.

8. have a shaved head. Many cultures believe this will help the hair to grow in thicker.

9. appear neglected—for example, diapers are not changed often enough; body is unwashed, and so on. This may be a result of parental stress and culture shock, especially if the family is used to having servants at home, or has never had modern washing conveniences—may not know how to access and/or use washing machines, and so on.

10. be inappropriately dressed. Some countries may not have central heat, or environmental conditions may be very different from those found in their new environment. Thus, indoor/outdoor clothing may be a concept with which they are unfamiliar. Children may have on many layers or may wear no socks or underwear. This is usually a reflection of the parents' unfamiliarity with the need for certain types of clothing.

Insect bites, hives that itch and cause the child to scratch self

Children with head lice sometimes have their heads shaved.

Family may not have the resources for proper diapers or appropriate clothing.

Abuse/Neglect

- Eliminate any possibility of child abuse and/or neglect.

- Learn about the customs/traditions of the child's culture. Invite the parents in for an informal discussion, and encourage them to explain and share their customs and/or traditions with staff.

- Accept individual and/or cultural differences working to help the child develop ways that can help him/her to be socially successful (appropriate gestures, key words and/or phrases).

- Do not overreact or tell the parents not to have the child's head shaved, for example. Try to be accepting in the manner in which staff interact with the parents.

- Be flexible in how different standards are accepted, interfering only if it is seriously harmful to the child or other children.

- Encourage parents to allow the child to bring a favorite toy, family picture, videos, picture books about their home country, and so on, to the center.

- If other children are ridiculing the child, try to explain to the other children about cultural differences, such as why a child might be dressed differently from themselves, or bring food that looks or seems strange to the other children.

- In working with the parents, try to change one thing at a time. Choose those problems that are most crucial to the child and the center.

11. lack dental/medical care. Some children, especially those from African/Asian countries, cannot tolerate cow's milk, hence they may suffer from lack of calcium. Refugee children may also have had long periods of malnutrition, which have affected the teeth.

SOCIAL/EMOTIONAL BEHAVIORS

The child may

1. show extreme anxiety on separation from the parent–shaking body, vomiting, gagging, injuring/hitting self or others, very stiff controlled posture, or an inability to move.

2. show less extreme, but equally uncontrolled screaming, kicking, throwing of objects, hitting, crying, or excessively passive (withdrawn) behavior.

3. be very depressed, passive, unresponsive, in shock, and/or have delayed responses.

4. lack comprehension of spoken English, and not make any attempt to listen or speak.

5. prefer to play alone, avoiding eye contact.

6. display emotions in a range of different ways, such as: very expressive, very uncontrolled, or very withdrawn.

7. have difficulty forming close relationships with teachers and peers.

Parents may not know that young children need dental care. They also may be unaware of how to access health and dental resources that may be available for their child.

Diet may be poor, or may have been poor over a period of time.

There may be an inherited tendency for poor teeth.

Behavioral/Social/Emotional Problems

Behavioral/Social/Emotional Problems (Oppositional Defiant Disorder [ODD])

Hearing Impairment

Speech and Language Problems

Autism Spectrum Disorder

Post-Traumatic Stress Disorder

The child may have experienced some trauma in the past–a death or having to leave someone he/she really cared about.

- Demonstrate activities that promote hygiene–programming them for the entire group–for example, brushing teeth, brushing hair, washing hands after using the bathroom, and so on.

- Explain individually to the parents about clothing, showing examples. Be prepared to be flexible and accepting.

- Clothing exchanges can be set up for families who have very limited resources.

- Accept attitudes about cleanliness that may be culturally determined. Be flexible, accepting different standards, only interjecting if the child's health or a breach of public health regulations is occurring.

- If too much tooth decay is evident, try to expand staff knowledge of what foods are rich in calcium and also acceptable in the culture from which the child comes. Try to obtain pamphlets on nutrition in the family's home language.

- Be sure that dental hygiene is a part of the regular school program. Consider inviting a dentist or dental hygienist to visit the program.

- Encourage the family of the child to have one of the parents stay with the child for a minimum of several days when the child starts the program. Be sure that separation is gradual and that the child is told when the parent is going to leave and return. First separation from the parent should usually be only 10 minutes, with a maximum of 30 minutes. The parent should

8. become dependent on one teacher, wanting to be held constantly; may violently reject other adults and children.

9. remain in one area of the room, exhibiting little initiative to play.

10. reject school food, clothing, toys, and so on.

11. react strongly to change in routines, room setup, field trips, and staff changes.

12. have few independent skills in self-help, such as feeding, toileting, dressing self, and may expect an adult to do this for him/her.

13. may not have been exposed to certain equipment and toys, such as climbing apparatus, tricycle, puzzles, lotto, and other matching games (may appear to have developmental delays).

14. have religious or cultural traditions that may restrict participation in certain activities.

SPEECH AND LANGUAGE CHARACTERISTICS

Children with English as a second language may have the following additional characteristics.

The child may

1. speak to others only in his/her home language and may assume that the other child/adult comprehends.

The child may be too tense to play, listen, or attend.

The child may not have had previous experience with toys and other equipment in the room. The food may be strange and unfamiliar to him/her.

Autism Spectrum Disorder
The child may have gone through numerous moves, often having to leave behind people with whom he/she has bonded.

Lack of experience

Intellectual Disabilities

then return to reassure the child. Be supportive of the child when the parent has left, explaining over and over that, for example, "Mommy will be back after snack," and point to the hands of the clock, or a pictorial timetable, and show the child when Mommy will return.

- Find out whether the child has older siblings in the school. Arrange for brief visits by the sibling if the child needs support.

- When the child is first starting the program, allow the parents to bring food from home for the child.

- The separation process is usually more traumatic and takes longer when the child does not understand the language used at the center.

- Encourage the parents to leave a glove, scarf, or something belonging to the parent that the child is most familiar with.

- Pictures of the child's family, pets, and so on are also helpful.

- When a child shows signs of depression and/or shock, he/she may need more physical contact from adults or siblings in order to be able to settle in.

- Work on developing relationship/body contact at a level the child can accept. If the child rejects or doesn't relax with contact, move away and comfort him/her with voice tone. Watch for signs of discomfort with voice tone. Watch for signs of discomfort with touch, and act accordingly.

2. not respond because a) the child does not recognize the pronunciation of his/her name; b) the voice intonation of the speaker differs from the child's speech.

3. echo words that others say (without comprehending).

4. not speak any English, but may comprehend a great deal of what he/she hears in English. It may take months before he/she begins to speak English.

5. use more nonverbal gestures than verbal language.

6. have difficulty with some sounds that are not common to his/her home language. Sounds not common in their home language may continue to be mispronounced for years.

7. feel uncomfortable when speaking to strange adults or children, even in his/her home language. Dialects may also differ.

SOCIAL ADAPTIVE BEHAVIORS

Children with English as a second language may have the following additional characteristics.

The child may

1. avoid confrontation, lack assertiveness, be passive, or be physically over assertive.

Autism Spectrum Disorder

The child may not have had the opportunity to learn social skills, or may have learned a different pattern of social skills.

- Use a lot of nonverbal language.

- Play near the child and try interacting through toys.

- Model appropriate, simple words in English, using consistent descriptive words—for example, do not say "shut the door" one time and "close the door" the next time.

- If teachers do not comprehend the child's home language, let him/her know through gestures what is expected.

- Demonstrate the meaning of words by using gestures and other augmentative communication methods (See **Cerebral Palsy: Augmentative Communication Systems**).

- Use games that encourage gestures.

- Develop activities that play with sounds, like animal and object noises. In singing and playing games, encourage the child to participate, but do not force him/her.

- Model useful body language for the child.

- Model the use of single words or short phrases, gesturing in order to clarify the meaning of your message. Realize that recognizing the meaning of a new word takes frequent exposure to the word and that it may take a great deal of time for the word to be learned.

- If the child is concerned about new people or situations, use gestures to reduce the amount of language.

2. avoid eye contact, physical or verbal contact with peers because he/she cannot communicate effectively.

3. tune out or daydream, particularly in situations when many words are used and/or there are few visual cues.

4. have difficulty understanding humor.

5. not respond to the teacher's directions, guidance, or limit-setting.

6. understand English better at some times than at others; comprehension can be influenced by tiredness, ill health, emotional upset, relationship to the speaker, speaker's accent and speaking style.

7. regress in language when there is a new teacher or a change in situations.

8. be comfortable speaking only with peers or only with one teacher.

9. become easily frustrated when others do not understand his/her speech.

10. use his/her home language in play, especially if there are other children who speak the same language.

Note: Those children who speak English with a dialect may at times have difficulty comprehending standard English as well as being understood by others when they speak.

Autism Spectrum Disorder

Hearing Impairment

Behavioral/Social/Emotional Problems

Hearing Impairment
Speech and Language Disorders

Essential Information

1. It is important that as children begin to learn English they do not lose their first language as this is the home language, the language that will bond them with their parents and other family members and friends. This bonding between the

- Try to arrange the schedule so that the child has only one or two major teachers. The staff can help the child to gradually develop play skills and interact with other children. When the child is more settled in, the teacher can begin to distance him-/herself more and share the responsibility with others.

- The staff *must follow the pace* of the child. The process of settling in may need to be very gradual.

- Find out from the parents the child's favorite toys, foods, and play activities, and incorporate these into the program.

- Include, with the support of the parents, pictures, books, objects, dress-up clothing, and so on, that reflect the family's country of origin.

- Gradually expand the child's play to incorporate other toys and activities, while still including the child's favorite toys and activities as a basic component.

- Model toy use and allow the child to observe others using "unfamiliar" equipment.

- Allow time for the child to observe others and then when appropriate, help him/her to enter play.

- The teacher may need to act as an intermediary between the child and others, helping to establish initial interaction for playing, introducing words and actions that help to model important social interaction tools, words like "mine," "May I play?"

child and parent is extremely important for his/her future social and emotional development.

2. There is evidence that the child who has developed a home language and retains and uses this home language will ultimately speak English more effectively because his/her brain is learning what a language is for, how it works, and how it is structured. This structuring in the brain is then more easily applied to learning another language.

3. Language is needed in order to think effectively. When we try to eliminate the child's first language, the language spoken in the home, we delay the development of thinking. It is therefore important to try to support the growth of the child's first language while introducing English, especially words that are needed in order for the child to communicate his/her needs and wants.

4. It is also important that the center respect and learn to understand the traditions and values of the culture from which the child comes. The staff should try to incorporate activities, materials, and so on from the child's home culture, encouraging the parents to contribute their knowledge to the program—for example, pictures, literature, videos, TV programs, music, dance, and so on.

5. Have the child's parents guide teachers in pronouncing the child's name; words used for Mommy and Daddy, siblings,

- When/if the child points, if necessary, model the appropriate word; when the child says the word, model the correct pronunciation in your next statements.

- Do not focus the child's attention on his/her error, or single the child out in any way. Praise all positive speech and language efforts. This will help to improve self-esteem.

- Initial interactions with children will be easier with only one or two others. Try to develop activities that facilitate this. The teacher may need to enter the child's play to model appropriate behavior.

- Sometimes there are one or two children in the group who have a higher degree of acceptance of others as well as, well-developed social skills. It is with one of these children that interaction with another child should be first initiated.

- Try to develop games and activities that require contact with peers and have simple repetitive speech; the teacher can enter play with the child when necessary, and then gradually withdraw from the interaction.

- Create group activities in which simple chants, songs, and games that incorporate difficult sounds are used. Encourage involvement in a nonintrusive way.

- Never laugh at the child, but do laugh with the child when recognizing something that the child sees as funny.

grandparents, and other family members, the bathroom, favorite foods, and so on.

6. If there is someone in the center who speaks the home language, it may be helpful to bring this person into the child's group as frequently as possible during the adjustment period.

- If there are a number of children who speak the same home language, allow them to play and talk in their language. Once the child is settled into the program, gradually create situations in which he/she is partnered with a child whose home language is English.

- Do not tell the child he/she must not speak in his/her home language, but encourage use of English words whenever possible.

- Do not force the child to eat school food. Try to find out the child's likes/dislikes in food; try to include foods he/she likes in the school menu.

- If staff changes occur, the new teacher should never force him-/herself on the child. Contact must be established slowly, smile, offer a familiar toy or favorite food.

- Reduce expectations. Introduce simpler toys and equipment usually used for slightly younger children.

- Try to break down tasks needed in self-help skills into small, easy steps. Try to reduce pressure to do self-help skills quickly.

- When/if the child is ill, overwhelmed, or upset, switch to activities that require less language.

In the center program:

- Provide toys that are easy to manipulate and control and provide immediate reinforcement–such as a music box or jackin-the-box. If the child is familiar with computer use, using the computer may be an excellent starting point.

- Encourage the child to try materials with which he/she can easily succeed, such as books, puppets, blocks/Lego building, cars, and trucks.

- Once the child has been in the program for a month or two, note specific areas in which he/she needs special help and try to develop program ideas that will foster needed skills and model appropriate actions.

- Try to work with the child in small groups, labeling objects, action words, and concepts, such as numbers, colors, sizes, shapes, and so on.

- Use pictures and puppets to show various emotions and to help the child label emotions.

- When making changes in the room, try to have the child present, even participating. Be sure he/she sees where his/her favorite activity or toys are being moved.

- Include multicultural literature. The child needs to see his/her culture reflected positively.

- When a child is having difficulty with another child—in a situation that demands communication—try to mediate, clarifying, interpreting, and providing visual clues.

RESOURCES

LOCAL

Board of education services, special support classes, and programs to support parents as well as children.

Library facilities–including computer access to programs that may help in second language development.

Some areas have resource centers and toy lending libraries from which parents might be able to access materials they cannot afford to buy.

Specific cultural groups may have centers, libraries, and/or museum exhibits that may help staff to understand more about the child's home culture.

UNITED STATES

National Clearinghouse for English Language
   Acquisition and Language Instruction
   Education Programs
2121 K Street NW, Suite 260
Washington, DC 20037
Tel: 1-800-321-6223
Online: http://www.ncela.gwu.edu

CANADA

Ministry of Citizenship
400 University Avenue, Suite 400
Toronto, Ontario M7A 2R9
Tel: 1-800-267-7329
Online: http://www.gov.on.ca/citizenship

ADDITIONAL RESOURCES

CURVATURE OF THE SPINE

Curvature of the Spine can be congenital (due to skeletal defects), hereditary, or caused by spinal injury usually prior to the age of three, sometimes older. It is more frequent in females than males.

Four types of spinal curvature are noticeable in childhood: scoliosis, lordosis, kyphosis, and congenital abnormalities of the spine.

Scoliosis refers to a curvature of the spine in which the normally straight vertical line of the spine is curved sideways. Scoliosis begins in childhood or adolescence and becomes progressively more pronounced until full growth is reached. Scoliosis is more common in females.

Lordosis refers to abnormally pronounced curvature of the spine ("sway back," "hollow-back"). Observable symptoms include the curved back and pronounced buttocks.

Kyphosis refers to abnormally pronounced hunched-over curvature of the top of the spine.

Congenital abnormalities of the spine may be noted first when one shoulder or hip seems higher than the other and/or when one leg appears shorter than the other, often affecting overall posture.

PHYSICAL AND BEHAVIORAL CHARACTERISTICS	Alternative Considerations and Conditions	Recommendations
Symptoms to look for may include: 1. any form of curvature of the spine–"swayback," skewed vertical posturing, pronounced protrusion of buttocks, or pronounced protrusion of the top of the spine. 2. unusual body stance. 3. unusual gait when walking or running. 4. poor balance or coordination in gross motor activities. 5. one hip or shoulder that appears to be higher than the other. 6. one leg that appears to be shorter than the other. 7. poor posture.	Weakness of the spine or muscles of the legs caused by **Muscular Dystrophy** ***Note:*** Young children often have a protrusion of the abdomen that creates the appearance of a sway in the back. However, as the child matures, the body posturing straightens. **Visual Impairment** **Hearing Impairment** Unusual posturing is at times associated with vision and hearing disorders in which the child has a deficiency in one side and postures so as to use the side that is functioning normally. Check the positioning of feet–is the child toeing in or out when walking and/or running?	• Monitor and record any related developmental delays. • Recommend that the child be sent for a medical assessment. Early identification of a spinal curvature may prevent long-term difficulty. • If any exercises or activities are recommended by the child's physician, the center staff should try to devise some games that are fun, and incorporate these into the regular program for participation by all the children.

8. overweight (causing back curving to compensate).

9. complains of back pain.

10. rib cage that appears to be deformed.

11. weak stomach muscles.

Intellectual Disabilities (Fragile X Syndrome)

Note: Make sure that the parents alert the center ahead of time of any medical procedures such as a cast or brace, so that teachers can develop a program that will help the child to cope more easily with the experience: books; dolls and puppets that can be "doctored"; medical vehicles–small for block and floor play, large for group dramatic play; and so on.

RESOURCES

LOCAL

Societies, associations, and organizations for scoliosis and lordosis

Spinal cord societies and associations

Local hospitals/clinics specializing in orthopedics

Orthopedic specialists

UNITED STATES

National Institutes of Health
National Institute of Arthritis and Musculoskeletal
    and Skin Diseases
1 AMS Circle
Bethesda, MD 20892-3675
Online: http://www.niams.nih.gov

Scoliosis Research Society
611 East Wells Street
Milwaukee, WI 53202
Tel: 1-414-289-9107
Online: http://www.srs.org

The Scoliosis Association, Inc.
P.O. Box 811705
Boca Raton, FL 33481-1705
Tel: 1-800-800-0669
Online: http://www.scoliosis-assoc.org

ADDITIONAL RESOURCES

CYSTIC FIBROSIS

Cystic Fibrosis is an inherited, chronic disorder that causes severe respiratory and digestive problems. In cystic fibrosis, the lungs and pancreas secrete thick and abnormal mucus, which blocks the respiratory tract, reducing the functioning of the nose and lungs. The digestive system and sweat glands are also affected.

It is important to know that the breadth and severity of impact of this condition will vary from child to child.

Cystic fibrosis is a genetic disease that is present at birth. It is most common among Caucasian people who are of northern and/or central European descent.

PHYSICAL CHARACTERISTICS	Alternative Considerations and Conditions	Recommendations
The child may have 1. a cough that hangs on and usually produces a large amount of sticky mucus. 2. wheezy breathing. 3. frequent respiratory infections (lungs, sinuses, and so on). 4. vomit that contains clear mucus. 5. unusual hunger. 6. loss of weight and/or failure to gain weight due to problems absorbing nutrients from food. 7. reduced growth rate. 8. weakness of muscles. 9. a lack of ability to sustain exercise. 10. a tendency to become lethargic. 11. abdominal pain/potbelly appearance. 12. a salty taste to his/her skin. 13. strong smelling bowel movements.	*Note:* Other possible causes of these or similar symptoms will be recognized in a medical assessment. Croup **Allergies** **Asthma** Pneumonia **Failure to Thrive** Celiac disease Other conditions causing digestive problems	• If an infant in the center exhibits these characteristics, and has not been diagnosed, have the parents arrange for a medical assessment. • Be sure to check with the child's physician with regard to any activity restrictions, ways in which to administer medication, and so on. • It is important to keep the lines of communication open between the center and the child's physician, as well as with any support agencies. • Find creative ways in which to include this child in all games and activities (even if he/she cannot actively participate)—for example, the scorekeeper in outdoor sports/games, handing out equipment and supplies, and so on. • Be prepared with alternate activities and projects he/she can be involved in if he/she needs to take it easy for a while.

Note: Children will usually come to the center prediagnosed. Because of this, it is important to know what questions to ask when the child enters the program.

IMPORTANT QUESTIONS TO ASK

1. What methods of therapy are being used—mist, breathing exercises, massage?

2. What medication and nutritional supplements is the child taking? What dosage is required? How often? What is the quantity of pills or medication?

3. Is the child able to take pills/medication on his/her own?

4. Is the child going to need any special therapy during school hours? If yes, what arrangements have been made and what environmental accommodations may be necessary?

5. If the child needs to expel mucus, does he/she know how to use a tissue and how to find an appropriate place in which to discard it?

6. Are there any special diet requirements?

7. Are there any special precautions to take to guard against infections?

8. Are there any cardiac (heart) symptoms/complications during a flare-up?

9. What is the child's physical activity level? Are there any limitations?

Essential Information

Because there are likely to be certain environmental/physical needs, it is important to consider whether or not the center is presently equipped to provide an effective program for this child.

Environmental adaptations may need to be taken.

- Can a humidifier be set up in the room if this is necessary?

- Is there an adult who can supervise all the pill taking /medication that may be necessary throughout the day?

- How can you make it possible for this child to stay indoors during damp/cold weather?

- In what ways can the staff adapt the program in order to allow for alternate programming if the child cannot keep up with the activity level?

- Can activity be minimized during hot weather?

- Is the staff prepared to handle an emergency if one should arise?

- Be accepting, treating this child as normally as possible. This child needs limits as much as any other child. He/she may not be used to being told he/she must—or cannot—do something.

- Remember, in an inclusive situation, the goal is to help the child become as much as possible an active and participating member of his/her peer group. The child with cystic fibrosis may need help in dealing with social/emotional problems resulting from prior experience and physical limitations that are caused by his/her condition.

- Ongoing communication and sharing of observations and information with the family are extremely important.

- Depending on the weather and the child's physical health, there will be times in which this child can be more actively involved and other times when he/she is more limited.

10. Which agency/ies or physician/s or other specialists are working with the child? Who is the specialist that can support the center in understanding and programming for this child?

- What government or other organizations are available that might offer additional physical and/or financial support, or special training for staff, suggestions and support with regard to adapting the environment to meet the specific needs of this child?

RESOURCES

LOCAL

Associations, foundations, and organizations for cystic fibrosis.

Community support groups.

Hospital services.

Pamphlets and other materials that might help to educate staff.

Check local pharmacies for pamphlets, videos, and so on.

UNITED STATES

Cystic Fibrosis Foundation
6931 Arlington Road
Bethesda, MD 20814
Tel: 1-800-344-4823
Online: http://www.cff.org

Cystic Fibrosis Worldwide
Online: http://www.cfww.org

CANADA

Canadian Cystic Fibrosis Foundation
221 Yonge Street, Suite 601
Toronto, Ontario M4S 2B4
Tel: 1-416-485-9149
Online: http://www.cysticfibrosis.ca

ADDITIONAL RESOURCES

DIABETES
(Juvenile Diabetes)

Juvenile Diabetes is a chronic, metabolic disorder that results from the body's inability to produce insulin, or enough insulin. Insulin is a hormone produced in the pancreas which is needed to process food efficiently. Lack of enough insulin results in high levels of glucose (blood sugar) that stays in the blood, rather than entering the body cells. Therefore, the body is unable to absorb sugar normally. This results in high glucose levels in the blood and urine. Additional insulin—administered at specified intervals (e.g., injection or implant)—is usually necessary as soon as the condition is identified.

Type 1 Diabetes is most commonly found in childhood or adolescence. It is characterized by a sudden onset in a previously healthy child.

Though the cause is unclear, genetic factors (seen in other members of the family) are frequently found.

Prognosis: Currently, there is no permanent cure for diabetes. Insulin therapy, diet, medication, and exercise can help to manage and control the disease. Uncontrolled diabetes can lead to additional serious health conditions, including: heart disease, kidney failure, seizures, blindness, and circulation problems.

PHYSICAL AND BEHAVIORAL CHARACTERISTICS	Alternative Considerations and Conditions	Recommendations
The child may 1. appear pale and/or thin. 2. have abnormal increased thirst and appetite. 3. experience sudden loss of weight. 4. be listless, easily fatigued. 5. urinate frequently. 6. become dizzy, sleepy, and occasionally may become unconscious. **Children may come to the center pre-diagnosed.**	Any of these physical and/or behavioral characteristics may indicate a physical infection or other types of chemical imbalance. When a cluster of these characteristics is noted, one should start to suspect diabetes, particularly if there is a rapid (within a few weeks) onset.	• Keep an ongoing record of any behaviors or symptoms. Indicate activities or situations which seem to precipitate the onset of the symptoms. When writing up an observation, be sure to include the date, time of day, and the specifics of the behaviors and circumstances. The teacher should initial the observation so that he/she can easily be contacted for further information. • If a child, has not been identified as having diabetes, and a staff member notices a sudden and dramatic appearance of any of these symptoms, report it to the parents and recommend that the child be tested and assessed immediately by a physician. • The child who has been diagnosed with diabetes should wear a Medic Alert bracelet.

IMPORTANT QUESTIONS TO ASK

1. Is the child on a special diet?

2. Is the child receiving insulin? If yes,

   - How often is this administered?

   - When is it administered?

   - By whom is it administered?

3. What steps should be taken if there is an insulin reaction?

4. Does the child's urine have to be tested? If yes,

   - How often?

   - By whom?

5. Is there a special fruit, juice, candy, or sweet that the child is used to receiving if an insulin reaction is suspected?

IMPORTANT INFORMATION

Insulin Reaction (Hypoglycemia)

Insulin reaction occurs if the child has received too much insulin, if insulin has been ingested too quickly by the body (perhaps from excess exercise), or if there has been inadequate caloric intake.

Essential Information

Early Symptoms of Insulin Reaction
- tremors
- sweating
- weakness
- dizziness
- pupils dilated
- numbness
- abnormal gait
- odd behavior
- restlessness
- skin pallor

- It is important to make sure the child has eaten breakfast.

- If a meal is delayed, or the group is going to take a trip, be sure you can provide the child with a snack.

- Be sure a sugar source is available at all times—when playing outdoors, going on trips, and so on.

- If possible, use the sugar source that the child is familiar with.

- Encourage normal activities, but regulate the amount of physical energy the child exerts at any given time.

- It is important to maintain a balance between food intake, exercise, and medication.

- The child's physician—with parental permission—should be consulted for guidance in the management of the child.

Recommendations for Insulin Reaction

If an insulin reaction is suspected, the child should **immediately** be given something containing sugar—fruit juice, a cube of sugar, or a piece of candy. This cannot harm the child and may prevent a severe reaction.

If the child does not improve within a few minutes after administration of sugar, take him/her to the hospital.

Late Symptoms of Insulin Reaction
- unconsciousness
- convulsions

If later symptoms are noted, the child should be taken to the hospital immediately.

RESOURCES

LOCAL

Associations, societies, and organizations for diabetes

Hospital services/clinics

Medic Alert bracelet information

UNITED STATES

American Diabetes Association
1701 North Beauregard Street
Alexandria, VA 22311
Tel: 1-800-342-2382
Online: http://www.diabetes.org

Juvenile Diabetes Research Foundation
  International
120 Wall Street, 19th Floor
New York, NY 10005-4001
Tel: 1-800-533-2873
Online: http://www.jdf.org

United States National Disease Information
  Clearinghouse
1 Information Way
Bethesda, MD 20892-3560
Tel: 1-800-860-8747
Online: http://www.niddk.nih.gov

CANADA

Canadian Diabetes Association
15 Toronto Street, Suite 800
Toronto, Ontario M5C 2E3
Tel: 1-416-363-3373
Online: http://www.diabetes.ca

Juvenile Diabetes Research Foundation
National Office
7100 Woodbine Avenue, Suite 311
Markham, Ontario L3R 5J2
Tel: 1-905-944-8700
Online: http://www.jdfc.ca

ADDITIONAL RESOURCES

EPILEPSY

Epilepsy is a disorder of brain functioning causing recurrent seizures. It is not a disease. It is a sign or symptom of a structural or chemical disorder that occasionally produces sudden electrical discharges within the brain. These, in turn, may cause seizures. There are many different kinds and levels of intensity of seizures. The two main categories of seizures that affect young children are **Tonic-clonic** (previously called grand mal), and **Absence seizures** (previously called petit mal). The Absence form of epilepsy often goes unrecognized, and the preschool or primary school teacher may be the first to recognize that a child has this disorder.

Seizures in Epilepsy may be generalized, affecting the whole body, or partial, the electrical discharge in the brain being limited to one area.

Note: A child who has epilepsy should wear a Medic Alert bracelet.

PHYSICAL AND BEHAVIORAL CHARACTERISTICS	Alternative Considerations and Conditions	Recommendations
• **Tonic-clonic seizures** (grand mal): This form of epilepsy is characterized by seizures in which there is often a loud cry, followed by a loss of consciousness and convulsive, rapid, and generalized uncontrolled body movements. The child will usually fall down as the seizure begins. He/she may froth at the mouth; the muscles may be jerking violently; and the child may lose bladder and/or bowel control. The seizure will usually last two to three minutes. The child will usually sleep for a while after having the seizure. After a seizure, a child will not remember what occurred during the seizure. He/she may be generally confused and disoriented. Sometimes children have side effects from drugs prescribed to curtail seizures. These side effects include drowsiness or hyperactivity.	Some children have learned how to bring on unconsciousness when having a tantrum, or when they are extremely angry or scared. The child may or may not have control over this behavior. Sometimes extreme allergic reactions to food or airborne substances will create a severe reaction. This reaction may take the form of a seizure. High fevers may at times be accompanied by seizures.	**Important Information to Find Out** Because the child with Tonic-clonic seizures will in most instances come to the center prediagnosed, it is important to know the general nature (pattern) of his/her seizures, such as duration or usual behaviors. Staff should also know • whether the child is on any medication. • any specific directions to follow if the child has a seizure. • whom to contact in case of an emergency. **If a seizure should occur:** • Try not to panic if the child has a seizure. Remain calm. Seizures cannot be stopped once they have begun. • Ease the child to the floor, if necessary, and loosen his/her clothing. • Place the child on his/her side to maintain a clear airway and prevent choking on the saliva or biting of the tongue.

Note: If a seizure should occur, contact the parents right away. If a child undergoes a series of seizures (one after another), seek medical assistance immediately. If this should occur, call an ambulance and take the child to the hospital.

- **Absence Seizures** (petit mal): This form of epilepsy is characterized by a brief loss of consciousness, lasting from 1 to 10 seconds.

  These seizures frequently begin between the ages of two and four, and usually stop at adolescence.

  The child may

  1. cease all activity.
  2. appear to be staring off into space, as if daydreaming.
  3. exhibit a series of muscle jerking and/or a brief loss of muscular control.
  4. smack or move his/her lips.
  5. blink, roll his/her eyes.
  6. after the seizure, usually resume his/her activity as if nothing had occurred.
  7. be unaware that he/she is having seizures. Because the child has never known any other way, he/she is probably totally unaware of the disability.
  8. be unable to answer questions appropriately because of the momentary lapses of consciousness, which result in him/ her receiving only bits and pieces of information during the seizure.

Hearing Impairment

Behavioral/Social/Emotional Problems

- Remove dangerous objects (chairs or tables with sharp corners) from the area to prevent accidental injury.

- Do not restrict the child's movements, except to prevent injury to the head and/or body—for example, try to put a soft object under the child's head to protect it from the hard surface of a floor or pavement.

- Do not insert any object between the teeth.

- Do not panic if the child seems to stop breathing momentarily.

- Explain to the other children that this child will be fine in a few minutes; that in every other way he/she is the same as they are; that this is something that he/she cannot control (like sneezing/coughing).

- Do not stand over the child with the group of children. When the child wakes, it is important that the re-entry into the group be as natural as possible.

- It is important to record
  - frequency of seizures.
  - when they are most likely to occur.
  - under what circumstances they are most likely to occur.

- Try to write a descriptive report of those behaviors that are observed. Your local Epilepsy Association may be able to provide the center with an appropriate form for recording.

9. not remember the seizure and may not realize anything unusual has happened.

Note: Because generalized absence seizures are often not recognized, it may also have been misdiagnosed as something else. Adults often think that the child is lazy or disrespectful, not realizing that the source of the behavior is absence seizures.

- **Partial or Psychomotor Seizure** is a form of epilepsy that is rarely found in young children. The seizure generally lasts two to five minutes and is followed by a period of amnesia.

Observable behaviors include

1. uncontrolled body movement.

2. inappropriate actions such as chewing, facial distortions, unaccountable, violent physical outbursts.

Other, less observable symptoms include

1. abdominal pains, headaches, buzzing in the ears, and dizziness.

2. chewing or lip-smacking.

Some children with **Behavioral/Social/ Emotional Problems, Autism, Tourette Syndrome**, and/or **Learning Disorders** have similar symptoms such as "tuning out" or unusual body movements.

Behavioral/Social/Emotional Problems

Tourette Syndrome

Undiagnosed medical problems, such as a brain tumor.

If Absence (petit mal) Seizures are suspected

- contact a local health official (or the child's physician) for advice on appropriate next steps to take.

- Try to maintain an accepting, positive reaction to the child. Whenever the child appears confused or bewildered, ignore the phasing out and try to repeat what has been said and/or explain some action that occurred.

- Seek to build and maintain an ongoing dialogue with the parents.

- Obtain directions to follow to meet the individual needs of this child, should a seizure occur.

- Try to include the child as fully as possible in the normal routine of the center.

- Try to avoid any known triggers.

- This child will need close supervision for swimming or on any climbing apparatus.

- It is helpful if the child gets enough sleep and eats balanced meals at regular intervals.

RESOURCES

LOCAL

Epilepsy associations, federations, societies

Clinics/hospitals; organizations on seizure and convulsive disorders

Medic Alert bracelet information

Check local pharmacies for pamphlets, videos, and other relevant resources.

UNITED STATES

American Epilepsy Society
342 North Main Street
West Hartford, CT 06117-2507
Tel: 1-860-586-7505
Online: http://www.aesnet.org

Epilepsy Foundation
4351 Garden City Drive
Landover, MD 20785-7223
Tel: 1-800-332-1000
Online: http://www.efa.org

CANADA

Epilepsy Canada
1470 Peel Street, Suite 745
Montreal, Quebec H3A 1T1
Tel: 1-877-734-0873
Online: http://www.epilepsy.ca

ADDITIONAL RESOURCES

FAILURE TO THRIVE (FTT)

Failure to Thrive (FTT) is most frequently used to describe a condition in an infant or toddler in which the only obvious symptom is a failure of physical growth and development; it is often accompanied by a disruption in psychosocial development. Failure to Thrive may have organic/biological or social/emotional roots.

Once it is established that a child has Failure to Thrive, all possible causes for the child's condition must be explored immediately.

- Organic causes of FTT include undiagnosed: kidney disease; intestinal problems causing malabsorption of nutrients; heart disease; HIV/AIDS, and maternal substance abuse.

- Nonorganic causes of FTT stem from underlying social and emotional problems, including: problems within the child's family—such as maternal deprivation or a faulty relationship between the primary caregiver and the child; poor or misguided parenting skills, or the possibility of abuse and/or neglect. Although Failure to Thrive is relatively rare, it is important to remember that it does exist. Special counseling and support are often required before the problem can be eliminated.

Nonorganic Failure to Thrive, as included in this section, should not be assumed as the cause of the child's condition, until organic causes of Failure to Thrive have been ruled out.

PHYSICAL AND BEHAVIORAL CHARACTERISTICS	Alternative Considerations and Conditions	Recommendations
The child may 1. have weight and height that are well below the expected norm. 2. fail to gain weight over a period of time. 3. exhibit delays, especially in fine and gross motor development, language and communication, and interactive and social skills. 4. be apathetic, irritable, lethargic, withdrawn; lack eye contact, and fail to respond appropriately (e.g., does not smile). 5. experience vomiting, diarrhea, recurrent respiratory infections, severe untreated diaper rash or cradle cap. 6. have thin hair, dark circles under the eyes, and/or enlarged abdomen.	Heredity–for example, are the parents small- or light-boned? Endocrine disorders such as lack of pituitary functioning or lack of thyroid gland functioning Anemic/iron deficiency **Fetal Alcohol Syndrome/Maternal Substance Abuse** **Intellectual Disabilities** **Heart Abnormalities** Developmental delay Diarrhea caused by intestinal problems **Nutritional Deficiencies** Failure of normal kidney functioning (can be from a urinary infection)	***Note:*** If a child, with no previous diagnosis of FTT is at the center, it is important to recommend that the parents take the child for an immediate, complete, medical examination. If this recommendation is not followed up, speak with the supervisor with regard to contacting Child Protective Services/Child and Family Services. - If the child is from another country he/she may not be adjusting to the climate or his/her immunities may not be sufficiently developed. The food served at the center may also be unfamiliar to the child. - If the parents seem open to suggestions, recommend books, parent support groups, and other resources that support parenting skills. - Be sure to check for dietary problems.

7. have a poor appetite.

8. not mold to the mother's body.

9. resist comforting.

10. sleep excessively.

11. not make vocal sounds—such as babbling noises.

12. relate inappropriately to strangers.

13. withdraw from parents or caregivers.

Cystic Fibrosis; Cultural Influences/ English as a Second Language/English with a Dialect
Autism Spectrum Disorder

Medical reaction from medication given for another condition
Prolonged hospitalization or isolation

Autism Spectrum Disorder
Intellectual Disabilities
Abuse/Neglect

- Keep an ongoing record of the child's behavior and development. Note anything that seems to deviate from the norm.

Note: Because individual issues causing Non-organic Failure to Thrive are almost always complex, a treatment plan usually requires the involvement of many qualified mental health professionals, such as pediatrician, nutritionist, dietitian, social worker, physiotherapist, occupational therapist, developmental psychologist, and/or psychiatrist.

RESOURCES

LOCAL

Hospitals, children's clinics, and social services for children and families

Pediatricians

Community service organizations and agencies

UNITED STATES

The Magic Foundation for Children's Growth
1327 N. Harlem Avenue
Oak Park, IL 60302
Tel: 708-383-0808
Online: http://www.magicfoundation.org

Foundation for Children with Special Needs
312 Stuart Street
Boston, MA 02116
Tel: 1-617-482-2915
Online: http://www.fcsn.org

ADDITIONAL RESOURCES

FETAL ALCOHOL SYNDROME (FAS)/
FETAL ALCOHOL EFFECT (FAE)/
MATERNAL SUBSTANCE ABUSE

Fetal Alcohol Syndrome (FAS) is a condition caused by maternal alcohol consumption during the pregnancy. It is a leading cause of intellectual disability (mental retardation). FAS causes a group of congenital defects in the infant. The damage to the central nervous system is permanent. It will not increase or decrease.

There is a cluster of characteristics that may be present at birth, including: prematurity, low birth weight, microcephaly (small head) or facial abnormalities. Other characteristics of FAS become more evident as the child develops. These include: over- or underactivity to touch, sound, sight, smell, and movement. Visual-spatial and auditory processing problems, as well as severe motor planning and sequencing problems may also occur. These will all range in severity.

Fetal Alcohol Effect (FAE) is a less severe condition, also caused by maternal alcohol consumption during pregnancy. It is often not noticeable at birth as these children do not have physical deformities. When the child enters the school system and intellectual deficits become evident, it is usually identified.

Maternal Substance Abuse is the term used when a mother has exposed her unborn fetus/child to alcohol and/or drugs—including prescription drugs, illegal drugs such as cocaine, crack, and heroin. Use of nicotine, caffeine, and/or over-the-counter drugs during pregnancy may also impact on the development of the unborn child.

Infants born to drug-addicted mothers are usually born addicted and have gone through a period of withdrawal at birth. Many of these infants are also born prematurely.

PHYSICAL CHARACTERISTICS	Essential Information	Recommendations
Congenital defects in children with FAS include: 1. small head and brain. The child is frequently permanently intellectually disabled. 2. facial abnormalities, including: • small eyes. • crossed eyes. • eyes wide spaced. • small, folded, eyelid openings. • short upturned nose; flat bridge. • thin upper lip. • small chin and jaw; flat cheekbones. • small or malformed teeth. 3. small stature; growth disturbances. 4. irregular body proportions.	Many of these children will come to the center previously diagnosed. Initial developmental assessments will have been completed, and the family will be involved with a social service agency, which can provide special guidance to the child's teachers as well. It is important that the teacher keep ongoing developmental records of the child's progress in the program. There may be children in the center who have not been previously identified. It is extremely important to work with the parents to find an agency that will guide the family and the teachers in providing the most beneficial learning experiences for the child.	**It is important to contact social service agencies if it is suspected that a child may have FAS/FAE or drug-related problems.** • Children with intellectual and behavioral problems often need more individualized program plans than most other children. Their needs include: –consistency of expectations with regard to behavior and social interactions. –realistic expectations with regard to self-help/care skills. The child may need to be taught how to do basic things–for example, button his/her shirt; put on shoes; wipe nose; cover mouth when coughing; and so on. If the child has never learned

5. poor muscle tone.

6. hearing defects/impairment.

7. cleft palate.

8. cardiac defects.

9. vision problems (nearsightedness).

BEHAVIORAL/SOCIAL/EMOTIONAL CHARACTERISTICS

Characteristics of children who have been affected by **Maternal Drug Abuse**–as well as those with **FAS/FAE** include:

1. being irritable and overly active in infancy.

2. being hyperactive, nervous, anxious, and/or impulsive

3. being withdrawn.

4. having attention deficits.

5. being hyperactive.

6. being easily distracted.

7. having processing problems–visual-spatial, auditory, and so on.

8. having poorly developed fine and gross motor skills.

9. having poor motor planning and sequencing problems.

10. having poor listening skills.

Children with FAS/FAE and other drug related damage will have lifelong, permanent difficulties. It is essential that a developmentally appropriate, specialized program be designed to help the child use his/her strengths and find ways to compensate and develop to his/her maximum potential.

Many children with FAS/FAE and drug-related problems experience learning, behavioral, and physical problems that children who have other conditions also experience. The main difference is that when the cause of the difficulties is known–FAS/FAE–the parents may blame themselves for the condition, and in turn may be overly solicitous, or be experiencing feelings of inadequacy as a parent.

Adoptive parents must also be aware that a child with FAS/FAE often experiences behavioral and learning problems that are congenital and not related to parenting.

these skills previously, it may take a lot of patience as one teaches him/her in a step-by-step manner how to do something.

–learning how to follow routines.

- It is also important to recognize the child's interests and strengths and to try to build on these in ways that will facilitate learning, as well as positive social experiences with other children in the group.

- Because many of these children have perceptual/motor problems, staff will have to be aware that the child may not recognize dangerous situations in outdoor gross motor play.

11. having developmental delays, learning disabilities, sensory integration dysfunction, attention deficit disorder, intellectual disabilities, and/or behavioral/social/emotional problems.

12. having poor speech development and poor language comprehension and communication skills.

13. experiencing temper tantrums, mood swings, and/or appearing withdrawn.

14. having difficulty following instructions or responding to limits.

15. displaying poor judgment.

16. lacking appropriate social skills with peers.

17. having inappropriate social interactions—for example, overly friendly, overly talkative, overly uninhibited.

RESOURCES

LOCAL

Hospital clinics.

Agencies that serve drug and alcohol addiction may be able to offer support or suggest local resources.

Child and Family Services/Children's Aid Agency.

UNITED STATES

Fetal Alcohol Syndrome Family Resource Institute
P.O. Box 2525
Lynnwood, WA 98036
Tel: 1-800-999-3429
Online: http://www.fetalalcoholsyndrome.org

March of Dimes
Online: http://www.modimes.com

Maternal Substance Abuse and Child Development
Online: http://www.emory.edu

CANADA

Canadian Centre on Substance Abuse
75 Albert Street, Suite 300
Ottawa, Ontario K1P 5E7
Tel: 1-613-235-4048
Online: http://www.ccsa.ca

Centre for Addiction and Mental Health
33 Russell Street
Toronto, Ontario M5S 2S1
Tel: 1-800-463-6273
Online: http://www.camh.net

National Birth Defects Prevention Network
Tel: 1-770-488-3550
Online: http://www.nbdpn.org

National Clearinghouse for Alcohol and Drug
    Information
P.O. Box 2345
Rockville, MD 20847-2345
Tel: 1-800-729-6686
Online: http://www.health.org

National Council on Alcoholism and Drug
    Dependence, Inc.
20 Exchange Place, Suite 2902
New York, NY 10005
Tel: 1-800-622-2255
Online: http://www.ncadd.org

National Institute on Drug Abuse
6001 Executive Boulevard, Room 5213
Bethesda, MD 20892-6432
Online: http://www.drugabuse.gov

National Organization on Fetal Alcohol Syndrome
216 G Street NW
Washington, DC 20002
Tel: 1-202-785-4585
Online: www.nofas.org

ADDITIONAL RESOURCES

GIFTED
(Intellectually Gifted and Talented)

A **Gifted** child is one who has advanced cognitive and developmental abilities. The label "gifted" covers a broad range from "mildly" gifted (advanced), to extremely gifted (advanced in all developmental areas), to gifted or talented in one or more areas. Young children who are gifted can be identified by their advanced abilities when compared with children of their same age. Their learning style is usually different from other children. Gifted children are found in all socioeconomic groups but may be more difficult to recognize in children who come from more culturally deprived backgrounds or who do not have English as a first language.

A **Talented** child has one or more specific special abilities—such as in music, art, mathematics, and so on.

Like all children, gifted and talented children may have social, emotional, behavioral, and developmental problems in some areas of learning and/or development.

PHYSICAL AND BEHAVIORAL CHARACTERISTICS	Essential Information	Recommendations
The child will often 1. grasp and understand new ideas quickly; have a keen general interest in a broad range of areas. 2. be curious, always seeking new knowledge, asking many intelligent questions, exploring new games, toys, objects, and experiences at length. 3. have a retentive memory (may remember things you wish he/she had forgotten). 4. be a leader among his/her peers; or may have a problem socializing with age-mates. **Note:** This lack of social interaction with peers may be caused by discontinuity of interests and impatience when peers comprehend things differently and/or more slowly.	Some children who are particularly talented or gifted in one specific area, such as art, music, or activities involving physical coordination, will need special support in further developing their abilities in these areas. The balance of how to support these special abilities while at the same time providing more standard programming in other areas is a challenge for the center. Some children of "average" intelligence may develop early in certain areas; however, the profile flattens out as the child matures. Examples include: early walking and early reading. Parents sometimes push children to excel, sending them to a multitude of programs, including a regimen of teaching their toddler to read, and so on. Though this may stimulate an interest in learning in some children, it may totally frustrate others, leading to fears of failure, and a "turning off" of interest in reading and/or math.	• Provide greater challenges in areas in which the child has shown advanced skill and understanding so that the child does not become bored—which can lead to withdrawn or acting-out behavior. • Try to provide open-ended activities and opportunities for the child to explore as far as he/she wants. Materials that can lead to expanding a project should be available if possible. • Try to have on hand additional and more complex equipment and materials that will facilitate more advanced exploration and learning. • Try not to restrict the child's development. Even though the teacher may have had one idea of how materials should be used, if the child is not misusing the materials, he/she should be allowed to explore and use them in unique ways.

5. develop speech and language early; have an advanced vocabulary, which continues to develop more quickly; learn new words and quickly incorporate them appropriately into his/her verbal communication.

6. have language development that is so sophisticated that the child may become frustrated when peers cannot understand him/her.

7. make up songs and stories that he/she sings and tells to others.

8. have superior conversation skills, as well as early development of a sense of humor.

9. enjoy being read to, be able to sit and attend to a story for a lengthy period of time, and be able to retain the content of what he/she has heard.

10. have advanced reasoning ability, as well as verbal and concrete problem-solving skills (e.g., good at doing puzzles, drawing, balancing blocks, and constructing complicated structures).

11. have advanced ability in early number concepts.

12. (usually) reach developmental milestones earlier than other children of his/her age.

13. have advanced fine and/or gross motor ability.

14. have advanced learning-to-learn skills.

Note: The child who achieves because he/she is pushed should not be confused with the child who learns these things on his/her own.

Older siblings often unintentionally influence the development of a young child. A bright, though not "gifted" child may have more advanced development in some areas as a consequence of this.

Some cultures spend a great deal of time developing certain skills. Therefore, these areas may be more advanced, even though the child may not be "gifted."

- Only where necessary should conformity be stressed—rules for safety, taking turns, sharing, and so on.

- Try to avoid situations that isolate or in some way undermine the child.

- Encourage and give support to the child in areas where he/she is least advanced. Remember, just because the child catches on quickly and explores openly in one area does not mean that he/she has the same ability in another.

- Because social development is extremely important in the early years, try to provide a broad scope of opportunities for learning, sharing, interpersonal involvement, and development of individual and group social interactions.

Some suggested activities include:

- card games and board games
- gross motor games like
  - dodge ball
  - "statues"—in which children move/dance as music is played and then must maintain their current position when the music stops
  - a variation of "musical chairs" in which the children are not eliminated, but must share chairs with each other as the chairs are removed one at a time when music is stopped

15. desire, accept, and carry out responsibilities; enjoy acting independently and become absorbed in challenging tasks and experiences.

16. demonstrate readiness to help peers who need support.

17. have taught self to read at an early age; or is learning to read and/or write from television. Frequently asks questions about letters, sounds of letters, numerals and quantity, and so on.

18. have a longer attention span and be able to handle frustrating situations more easily than most of his/her peers.

19. be a keen observer.

20. be more advanced and become bored with routine tasks, repetitive programs, or with activities that are still of interest to peers but are not challenging intellectually or physically to him/her (this sometimes leads to acting out and attention-getting behavior).

21. be self-motivated, creating new games, activities, experiments, and experiences.

22. learn a second language much faster than peers.

23. have an area in which the child excels— for example, in psychomotor ability, art and/or music, abstract reasoning, and so on.

Important Considerations

At times, a child who is gifted may

- develop/exhibit signs of nervous tension, such as tics, speech hesitations (his/her thoughts may be faster than speech), leg movements, twitches.

- develop a behavior problem because he/she is bored with the pace of learning or content covered is already known to him/her.

- withdraw into his/her own thoughts and/or appear inattentive. Gifted children can often do more than one thing at a time without inhibiting the level of learning that occurs.

- be oversensitive to criticism.

Note: Gifted children are used to achieving with a high level of success and may find it difficult to receive/consider suggestions about alternative ways of trying something.

- Use of computers with young children must be carefully monitored. This is particularly true with children who have a longer attention span and may get so involved in computer play that if they are not given some limits, it may impact on their opportunities to develop physical and social interaction skills with peers.

- Appropriate computer programs for all young children, but especially for those who are advanced in their ability, should be open-ended and encourage creative problem solving—such as creating a story line, pictures, and/or designs. There are also excellent programs for learning phonics and early word attack skills, as well as classification and number problem solving skills. The major goal is to try to pick a program that is self-correcting and that is both enjoyable and challenging.

RESOURCES

LOCAL

Boards of education or special/enriched programs.

Organizations for "bright" children.

Opportunities to enrich the child's learning experiences–interactive art and science museums, art groups, music and drama groups that might offer programs and/or visit the center, and so on.

Community enrichment programs.

Note: Some larger cities have special classes and/or schools for gifted and talented children. Check with your Board of Education to find out what might be available.

UNITED STATES

National Association for Gifted Children
1707 L Street NW, Suite 550
Washington, DC 20036
Tel: 1-202-785-4268
Online: http://www.nagc.org

National Foundation for Gifted and Creative
   Children
395 Diamond Hill Road
Warwick, RI 02886-8554
Tel: 1-401-738-0937
Online: http://www.nfgcc.org

Council for Exceptional Children
1110 North Glebe Road, Suite 300
Arlington, VA 22201
Tel: 1-703-620-3660
Online: http://www.cec.sped.org

CANADA

The Association for Bright Children of Ontario
Box 156, Suite 100
2 Bloor Street West
Toronto, Ontario M4W 2G7
Tel: 1-416-925-6136
Online: http://www.kanservu.ca/~abc

Gifted Childrens Association of B.C.
210 West Broadway, 3rd Floor
Vancouver, British Columbia V5Y 3W2
Tel: 1-877-707-6111
Online: http://www.gcabc.ca

Gifted Canada
Online: http://www3.telus.net/giftedcanada

ADDITIONAL RESOURCES

HEARING IMPAIRMENT
(Intermittent, Partial Loss, or Permanent Hearing Loss)

A child with a **Hearing Impairment** usually exhibits deficits in language (receptive and expressive) and speech production. The amount of deficit depends on the type and degree of hearing loss. Impairment may be temporary, due to illness such as ear infection, or permanent—caused by congenital factors—such as malformation of the inner ear (cochlea), the auditory nerve, or the outer or middle ear. Children may also lose hearing through illness or injury.

The degree of developmental damage depends on the severity of the hearing loss and the age at which the hearing problem occurred.

HEARING IMPAIRMENT: PREVIOUSLY IDENTIFIED

ESSENTIAL INFORMATION AND IMPORTANT QUESTIONS TO ASK	Important Considerations	Recommendations
If a child with an identified hearing problem is entering the program, it is important to seek advice from the therapist and/or physician working with the child. 1. How long has the child had the impairment and at what age was it identified? 2. Does the child have any hearing? If yes, it is important to get ideas on how to maximize what hearing he/she has. 3. Find out what method of treatment has been established. Some specialists advocate using all residual hearing, others put emphasis on sign language, and many try to use a combination of maximizing hearing and signing. 4. What is the level of expectation one should have for this child? 5. Is the child on any medication–antibiotics and/or has he/she undergone any surgery–for example, for placement of tubes in the ears; and so on? The teacher may need to help prepare the child for	*Note:* The following points can be applied to most situations in which there is a child with special needs in the family. In seeking information from parents and specialists, it is important to be sensitive to emotional situations and experiences that may be influencing the current situation. For example: • The parents may blame themselves for the child's condition if the hearing impairment is due to the mother having had Rubella (German Measles) during pregnancy. • The parents may have experienced a great deal of frustration; they have been through years of trying to find cures, medical miracles, and new devices to help their child. • Parents have often done their own research into alternate treatments and educational goals. Some of these may be more realistic than others for their child. It is important to be empathetic and try to understand what the parents have been experiencing. Try to be open and accepting of their chosen position.	• It is important to do ongoing formal and informal observations and keep a running record. This should be shared on an ongoing basis with the parents. It is also important to make sure the parents share with the center what they are observing and experiencing at home. It is often helpful to have a journal (communication book) that goes back and forth between the school and the home with each party recording the child's experiences, including: new words used, new strategies tried, ways in which he/she did/did not participate in ongoing activities, and any other helpful information. • Try to note whether the child becomes tense, passive, or avoids certain situations. • At group time, seat the child across from the teacher, giving the child the best possible position for lipreading.

87

hospitalization (setting up a medical center play area, reading stories about going to the hospital, and so on).

6. If the child has hearing aids, the teachers must learn to
   - change batteries.
   - clean hearing aids.
   - adjust hearing aids if they malfunction.
   - adjust the ear mold for the child.
   - recognize a switched-off device (when children first start to wear hearing aids, it may take time for them to become accustomed to sound).
   - wear a special microphone around the neck that helps the child to hear more effectively what the teacher is saying.

- Be aware of personal biases. Seek additional information from parents and physicians that will help staff to become more familiar with the goals and objectives of the program they are advocating.

- Be aware that teachers have this child in the program for a given period of time. For parents, a child with special needs is an ongoing, often frustrating, day-after-day responsibility.

- Only some of the expenses involved in managing the care of a child with special needs are covered by insurance, special organizations, and government programs. Parents often have had to use their own resources (financial and otherwise), when traveling to specialists for advice, seeking the latest information about a condition, and/or joining organizations, seeking personal support, and so on.

- It is best if the teacher faces the light when talking with the child. It is best if the light is on the teacher's face, helping the child to see the teacher's mouth and facial expression most effectively.

- To get the child's attention, use gentle touches and eye contact to guide him/her to focus on the teacher, and/or the task at hand.

- Use as many visual aids as possible: holding up objects, using gestures, and demonstrating how something is used, while talking about it.

- In music activities, help the child to touch and experience the vibration in drums, pianos, and so on.

HEARING IMPAIRMENT: NOT PREVIOUSLY IDENTIFIED

PHYSICAL CHARACTERISTICS	Alternative Considerations and Conditions	Recommendations
The child may 1. have discharge from the ears. 2. have earaches and/or complain of crackling noises. 3. frequently rub his/her ears a lot. 4. breathe through his/her mouth. 5. complain of feeling dizzy. 6. complain of ringing or buzzing in his/her ears.	Ear infections **Allergies** Objects in the ear Swollen adenoids Flu Vision problems	• Check and make sure that the child has had a recent hearing assessment. • Many hearing problems in childhood are temporary—due to infection, wax buildup, allergies, and so on. If staff suspect that a child is having trouble hearing, explain this to the parents and encourage them to arrange for a medical checkup and hearing assessment. If the family does not follow

BEHAVIORAL CHARACTERISTICS

The child may

1. lack attention; daydream; "space out."

2. not follow directions; ignore or confuse spoken requests or directions.

3. have poor or delayed social skills; be withdrawn, seem overly shy, or have aggressive/explosive behavior.

4. have poor balance.

5. turn or tilt head to one side (toward sound).

6. ask for instructions to be repeated, or answer questions inappropriately.

7. substitute, omit, or distort certain sounds when speaking.

8. have poor articulation and/or grammar.

9. complain of not being able to hear.

10. respond to some sounds/tones and not to others.

11. seem to be imitating or picking up clues from others.

12. use hands excessively when talking.

13. have a voice tone that is often inappropriate; is monotone; is too loud or too soft; poor modulation of different tones; be hoarse or nasal.

14. request that a tape player, television, video player, and so on, be turned louder.

Autism Spectrum Disorder

Speech and Language Problems
Visual Impairment

Behavioral/Social/Emotional Problems

Motor Problems

Visual Impairment

Some sounds are more difficult if a child's first language is not English.
Cultural Influences on Behavior/English as a Second Language/English with a Dialect

Speech and Language Problems

The child may hear at some frequencies and not at others.

Autism Spectrum Disorder

Behavioral/Social/Emotional Problems

up, ask the family for permission to talk with the child's physician.

- Poor or minimal hearing in a young child has a direct impact on the development of speech/language.

- For this reason it is very important that any hearing problem be attended to as soon as it is recognized.

- If a child has a history of recurring frequent ear infections, observe closely for signs of hearing impairment. A hearing test could be beneficial, even if a mild degree of hearing loss is suspected.

- Try to obtain eye contact when interacting with the child.

- When a child does not respond to a verbal request, use touch to get his/her attention.

- In small group activities, team the child with a verbal classmate.

- Use visual clues such as real objects, pictures, and felt boards to reinforce what teachers are saying.

- Use many gestures to reinforce verbal messages.

- Get down to the child's physical level.

- Use the child's name when addressing him/her–"John, bring the red apple."

- Be sure to speak clearly.

- Give simple, concise directions.

- Try to face the child when talking to him/her. In group situations position the child so that his/her better ear is facing the speaker.

- Use simple language.

- Encourage dramatic play and social interaction.

- Wait for the child to speak or respond to questions before providing those words that he/she is not able to produce.

- In responding to the child, the teacher should model correct syntax and correct pronunciation.

- Do not pressure the child to repeat. Avoid making the child feel self-conscious.

- Make up games in which all the children can participate, especially games that will aid this child in practicing certain sounds.

- Use puppets, felt boards, and other visual aids to encourage language and social interaction.

See **Augmentative Communication Systems** under **Cerebral Palsy.**

RESOURCES

LOCAL

Community programs for the hearing impaired

Hospital audiology and speech clinics

Ear, nose, and throat doctors

Organizations that will screen young children for hearing deficits

Look for agencies that provide augmentative communication systems–for example:
  Sign Language
  Bliss Symbolics
  Picture boards
  Picture Exchange Communication Systems
    (PECS)

School boards and consultants for special services and speech/language support

UNITED STATES

Alexander Graham Bell Association for the Deaf
3417 Volta Place NW
Washington, DC 20007
Tel: 1-202-337-5220
Online: http://www.agbell.org

American Hearing Research Foundation
8 South Michigan Avenue, Suite 814
Chicago, IL 60603-4539
Tel: 1-312-726-9670
Online: http://www.american-hearing.org

American Society for Deaf Children
P.O. Box 3355
Gettysburg, PA 17325
Tel: 1-800-942-2732
Online: http://www.deafchildren.org

Deafness Research Foundation
1050 17th Street NW, Suite 701
Washington, DC 20036
Online: http://www.drf.org

National Association for the Deaf
814 Thayer Avenue
Silver Spring, MD 20910-4500
Tel: 1-301-587-1788
Online: http://www.nad.org

National Institute on Deafness and Other
  Communication Disorders
National Institutes of Health
31 Center Drive, MSC 2320
Bethesda, MD 20892-2320
Online: http://www.nidcd.nih.gov

CANADA

Canadian Association of Speech-Language
  Pathologists and Audiologists
401-200 Elgin Street
Ottawa, Ontario K2P 1L5
Tel: 1-800-259-8519
Online: http://www.caslp.ca

Canadian Hard of Hearing Association
2435 Holly Lane, Suite 205
Ottawa, Ontario K1V 7P2
Tel: 1-800-263-8068
Online: http://www.chha.ca

Canadian Hearing Society
271 Spadina Road
Toronto, Ontario M5R 2V3
Tel: 1-416-928-2500
Online: http://www.chs.ca

The Hearing Foundation of Canada
330 Bay Street, Suite 1402
Toronto, Ontario M5H 2S8
Tel: 1-800- 432-7968
Online: http://www.hearingfoundation.ca

Western Institute for the Deaf and Hard of
  Hearing
2125 West 7th Street
Vancouver, British Columbia V6K 1X9
Tel: 1-604-736-7391
Online: http://www.widhh.com

ADDITIONAL RESOURCES

Congenital Heart Defects are abnormalities of the heart or blood vessels that exist at the time of birth. They are one of the most common birth defects.

Some congenital heart abnormalities disappear as the child matures. The more serious defects usually require corrective surgery.

The causes of most defects are unknown. Possible causative factors include:
- maternal drug substance abuse.
- genetics.
- premature/preterm babies.
- infections/diseases in the early stage of pregnancy—for example, Rubella (German measles)
- chromosome disorder (e.g., Down Syndrome)

The prognosis, because of improved surgical procedures, is positive. Because of this, most children with heart abnormalities will be able to lead normal, active lives.

Note: If a child in the center sustains a mouth injury, it is important for the parents to be informed immediately. There is a condition called Bacterial Endocarditis that is caused by bacteria that enter the bloodstream. These bacteria settle in the lining of the heart, and if the child is not treated, the consequences can be serious. Antibiotics are given to prevent this condition.

PHYSICAL AND BEHAVIORAL CHARACTERISTICS	Alternative Considerations and Conditions	Recommendations
The child may 1. have skin, fingernails, lips, tongue, or toes that are bluish in color. 2. be unusually tired. His/her physical activity may be limited. 3. have shortness of breath, which may lead to difficulties in feeding, especially in infants and younger children. 4. have chest pains, dizziness, or fainting spells. 5. have physical growth or development that is behind the norm for his/her age. 6. be more susceptible to lung infections and infections to the lining of the heart.	Circulation problem Iron deficiency Lack of sleep **Nutritional Deficiencies** **Asthma** **Allergies** **Epilepsy** **Cystic Fibrosis** **Kidney and Bladder Disorders** Prenatal or postnatal injuries Inherited genetic malformations	• Be sure to obtain a note from the child's physician indicating any limitations. • If the child indicates that he/she is tired or dizzy, or appears pale, have him/her spend a quiet time with a book or table toy. • Do not isolate the child unless he/she appears to need sleep or rest. • Try to include the child in all activities that do not seem to overtire him/her. • If a previously undiagnosed heart problem is suspected, a general medical checkup for the child should be recommended to the parents.

Children may come to the center pre-diagnosed.

1. What is the child's physical level of activity? What can/can't he/she physically participate in at this time?

2. Are there any restrictions/limits that need to be imposed? If yes, what, when, for how long?

3. Does this child need more rest than other children? Does he/she need rest periods after extensive physical activity? Should physical activity be spaced with rest periods in between? Does the child indicate when he/she needs rest, or does he/she need to be monitored?

4. Are there any special exercises or activities that would be particularly helpful? If yes, what, how much, how long?

5. Are there any special precautions that need to be taken with respect to health—for example, regarding possible infections or certain foods?

6. Is the child taking medication? What is the dosage? Will the center need to administer any? Are there any side effects?

7. What should be done if an emergency should arise? Who should be called, contacted?

Fetal Alcohol Syndrome (FAS)/Fetal Alcohol Effect (FAE)/Maternal Substance Abuse

Note: In some cultures, physical activity is discouraged. The preschool or young elementary school child may be out of condition, hence the shortness of breath and feeling fatigued after exercise occurs.

Note: If there are any concerns, the center should share them with the parents and/or the child's physician.

- A record of the child's previous medical history should be in the child's file.

- Try to follow the recommended program without excluding the child from normal peer participation. In active games, try to create an inactive role if the child needs a quieter time. He/she could record scores, be the referee or umpire, be in charge of equipment, hold a rope, and so on.

- Do not overprotect the child. Encourage participation except as specifically prohibited.

- Be sure to record any behaviors or incidents that occur, indicating date, time, place, and circumstances under which the situation occurred.

- Be sure to have a "what to do in an emergency" system well established with all staff informed, and procedures posted in case a substitute staff person should be present.

8. Are there any specific symptoms that need monitoring?

9. Are there any secondary related problems?

10. Are there any other specifics that have not been covered in these questions?

RESOURCES

LOCAL

Hospital clinic services

Chapters of American Heart Association

Medic Alert bracelet information

UNITED STATES

American Heart Association
National Center
7272 Greenville Avenue
Dallas, TX 75231-4596
Tel: 1-800 242-8721
Online: http://www.americanheart.org

Congenital Heart Information Network
1561 Clark Drive
Yardley, PA 19067
Tel: 1-215-493-3068
Online: http://www.tchin.org

National Association for Children's Heart Disorders
1578 Careful Drive
Green Bay, WI 54304-2941
Tel: 1-800-538-5390
Online: http://www.kidswithheart.org

National Heart Lung and Blood Institute
Division of Heart and Vascular Diseases
Two Rockledge Center, Suite 9160
6701 Rockledge Drive
Bethesda, MD 20892-7940
Tel: 1-301-251-1222
Online: http://www.nhlbi.nih.gov

CANADA

Heart and Stroke Foundation of Canada
222 Queen Street, Suite 1402
Ottawa, Ontario K1P 5V9
Tel: 1-888-473-4636
Online: http://www.heartandstroke.ca

The Magic Foundation for Children's Growth
1327 N. Harlem Avenue
Oak Park, IL 60302
Tel: 1-708-383-0808
Online: http://www.magicfoundation.org

ADDITIONAL RESOURCES

HEMOPHILIA

Hemophilia is a disorder that is due to abnormal genes that in most instances are genetic. This is a condition that causes excessive bleeding due to a deficiency of the blood clotting protein factor. Hemophilia A and B occur almost always in boys. Hemophilia C (which is extremely rare) can occur in both boys and girls.

SPECIFIC CONSIDERATIONS

A child with hemophilia will usually come to the center prediagnosed. It is important to know signs to look for in this individual child.

Teachers should be aware of the extent of the problem. Some children have more severe conditions than others.

1. A slight scratch may lead to bleeding that cannot be stopped; a deep cut, a skin-bite, any incidents that involve bleeding may be problematic.
2. A child with hemophilia may bleed internally as a result of minor bumps and bruises, as well as from extra stress on certain muscles.

Signs of possible problems from internal bleeding are
- sudden swelling.
- joint pain and increased warmth to an area.
- stiffness.
- muscle weakness.
- bruises.
- headaches.
- unusual pupil size.
- grogginess.
- nausea.
- vomiting.

Essential Information

Because there are certain physical, as well as environmental needs, it is important to think about ways in which staff will need to adapt the environment in order to provide effective care for this child.

Continuous supervision on the playground and in gym activity will be necessary.

Explain to other children that this child has some special needs, but in every other way he/she is the same as they are. Remember, the child with hemophilia looks and has the same developmental needs as every other child; therefore, it may be harder for him/her to accept his/her limitations. Try to avoid situations that may create teasing.

A preset plan is needed so that if any emergency should arise, staff can immediately move into action. This may include getting the child to the hospital immediately.

Determine how much support the parents may need. It is important to find out whether there are community groups or organizations in the area that can help to support this family.

Recommendations

- Check the environment for any sharp corners of shelves or tables. Cover these with padding.
- Work with the child, helping him/her to recognize areas of potential danger, such as places where other children may be jumping down or objects that might topple. Try to find ways that the child can be alerted to danger areas; perhaps a colorful dot or mark that the child can learn to recognize as a clue.
- Make sure that the child lets staff know if anything does happen to him/her, such as a fall, bump, or scratch.
- Many children with hemophilia already know their limitations and how to avoid trouble spots; some may be overanxious, and staff may need to find ways to help the child relax.
- Work on developing nondangerous activities that can build social interactions, such as cognitive and creative activities, science and language, puppets, felt board, doll house with contents, and so on.
- Swimming and walking are good sports. Try to avoid all contact games/sports.

- dark brown urine (blood in urine).
- dark brown bowel movement (blood in bowel movement).
- abdominal pain.
- slurred speech.
- disorientation.
- prolonged bleeding after a minor injury or minor surgical or dental procedure.

IMPORTANT QUESTIONS TO ASK

It is extremely important to know what questions teachers need to find answers to when considering the implications of having a child with hemophilia in the center.

1. What is the range of problems that this child experiences?

2. How active does the child tend to be?

3. Is the child aware of the ways in which he/she might have to limit physical activity?

4. If the child bumps into an object or falls, what type of medical or other action is required?

5. Does the child need to wear any type of protective clothing, or use any type of protective equipment during play- such as a helmet or sponge rubber pads on the knees and buttocks?

6. Who should be contacted in case of a medical emergency? The center must have the name and phone number of the child's doctor, hospital, and specific course of action that needs to be followed if an emergency occurs.

It is important to monitor the child's activities and develop a note-exchange system with the parents.

Some children may be receiving treatment with blood clotting substances. These children do not need as much special monitoring. Get a report from the child's physician.

In preschool programs, *check your legal position if an accident should occur.* A written release from the parents may be required.

- Regular dental care is necessary to avoid the risk of bleeding from inflamed gums.

- Invite a medical specialist to the center to support and inform staff. Have this person look over the environment and make suggestions and recommendations.

- **The child with hemophilia should never be given aspirin.**

- The child should always wear a Medic Alert bracelet.

RESOURCES

LOCAL

Hospitals/clinics (find out specific services they offer)

Associations, foundations, societies, and organizations for hemophilia

Medic Alert bracelet information

UNITED STATES

National Hemophilia Foundation
116 West 32nd Street, 11th Floor
New York, NY 10001
Tel: 1-800-424-2634
Online: http://www.hemophilia.org

CANADA

Canadian Hemophilia Society
652 President Kennedy Avenue, Suite 1210
Montreal, Quebec H3A 1K2
Tel: 1-800-668-2686
Online: http://www.hemophilia.ca

World Federation of Hemophilia
1425 Rene Levesque Boulevard West, Suite 1010
Montreal, Quebec H3G 1T7
Tel: 1-514-875-7944
Online: http://www.wfh.org

ADDITIONAL RESOURCES

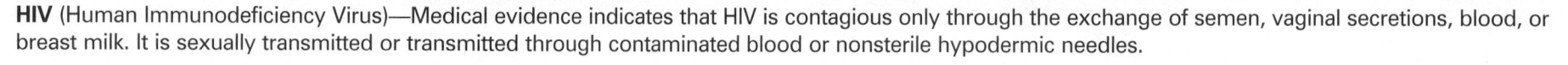

HIV-AIDS

HIV (Human Immunodeficiency Virus)—Medical evidence indicates that HIV is contagious only through the exchange of semen, vaginal secretions, blood, or breast milk. It is sexually transmitted or transmitted through contaminated blood or nonsterile hypodermic needles.

The majority of children with the HIV virus are infected by the mother during the time in which she was pregnant with them, giving birth, or breast-feeding. *Not all children with HIV will develop AIDS.*

AIDS (Acquired Immunodeficiency Syndrome)—AIDS is a syndrome that is caused by a virus commonly referred to as HIV. This virus attacks the body's immune system and leaves the individual vulnerable to infections or cancers.

Other children have acquired HIV/AIDS from contaminated blood transfusions (often required during surgery or organ transplants). Children with hemophilia and certain types of anemia that require repeated blood transfusions are at greater risk.

PHYSICAL AND HEALTH PROBLEMS	Essential Information	Recommendations
Children with HIV infection or AIDS have 1. extremely low resistance to all viruses, colds, pneumonia, and other infections. 2. persistent fatigue and/or unexplained weight loss. Other symptoms that are presently considered diagnostic markers of HIV/AIDS are • developmental delays/disabilities/disorders. • kidney and heart problems. • frequent staphylococcus, salmonella, and yeast infections. • sinus and ear infections. • flulike symptoms. • abdominal swelling. • itchy skin rashes. • frequent diarrhea.	Current research is indicating that HIV/AIDS is not transmitted through casual contact. **It is important to know that all of the symptoms found in HIV/AIDS are also found in many other common childhood infections.** Do not jump to conclusions that may be unfounded. *Note:* The HIV/AIDS virus dies very quickly if it is exposed to air. For this reason, AIDS cannot be contracted from • touching. • kissing. • coughing. • sneezing. • sharing drinking glasses. • door knobs. • toilet seats. • swimming pools.	• If a child with HIV/AIDS is referred to the center, get a written, signed statement of procedures, including essential information from the child's physician. • Follow the usual precautions taken for avoiding the spread of any germ or infectious condition when cleaning up or diapering a child with HIV. • Use rubber/protective (nonabsorbent) gloves while changing diapers, cleaning up vomit, or attending to an open wound. • If the child has vomited or bled on toys or rugs, wash them with a disinfectant before they are used by other children. • In a toddler/infant center, toys that are frequently mouthed should be washed each day with disinfectant.

- thrush (white coating on tongue) and/or enlarged lymph glands in the neck, armpits, and/or groin.
- night sweats or fevers.

Note: Kaposi's Sarcoma (a type of skin cancer that attacks the inside of the mouth and internal organs–e.g., lungs) is common in adults with AIDS, but is not common in young children with AIDS.

Remember: There should be a cluster of symptoms before one comes to the conclusion that a specific condition might exist.

Remember: All of the physical and health problems found in the left-hand column are frequently found in other childhood illnesses.

- Older children may tire more easily, and the program may need to be adapted in order to accommodate their specific needs.

Though many other things can cause all of these symptoms, if there is a cluster of the symptoms (mentioned in the left-hand column) observed, it is recommended that the child have a complete medical examination.

RESOURCES

LOCAL

Centers for Disease Control

Departments of Education

Departments of Health

AIDS Hotlines, United States and Canada

UNITED STATES

The CDC National AIDS Clearinghouse
P.O. Box 6003
Rockville, MD 20849
Tel: 1- 800-458-5231
Online: http://www.cdc.gov/hiv

National Institutes of Health
9000 Rockville Pike
Bethesda, MD 20892
Online: http://www.nih.gov

The Office of HIV/AIDS Policy
Online: http://www.osophs.dhhs.gov/aids

CANADA

Bureau of HIV/AIDS
Health Canada
Tunney's Pasture
Ottawa, Ontario K1A 0K9
Tel: 1-613-957-2991
Online: http://www.hc-sc.gc.ca

Canadian AIDS Society
309 Cooper Street, 4th Floor
Ottawa, Ontario K2P 0G5
Online: http://www.cdnaids.ca

Canadian HIV/AIDS Clearinghouse
1565 Carling Avenue, Suite 400
Ottawa, Ontario K1Z 8R1
Tel: 1-877-999-7740
Online: http://www.clearinghouse.cpha.ca

ADDITIONAL RESOURCES

INTELLECTUAL DISABILITIES
(Mental Retardation)

The term **Intellectual Disabilities** is used to describe a child whose intellectual functioning level and adaptive skills are significantly below the average for a child of his/her chronological age. Areas of significant developmental disability may occur in social, emotional, communication, physical, and/or functional academic skills. There is a wide range of differences in individuals with an intellectual disability. A mild or moderate intellectual disability may not be diagnosed until a child enters grade school and is required to demonstrate academic skills. Most individuals display specific areas of strength accompanied by other areas of development that need a great deal of support.

Children with more severe intellectual disabilities and adaptive skills often have additional physical and/or emotional/social disabilities that often necessitate specialized programming.

Intellectual disabilities can be caused by chromosomal or genetic disorders; injuries or illnesses that may occur prenatally or postnatally, as well as pre- or postnatal environmental conditions that impact on the development of the fetus or young child. It is often difficult to cite a specific single cause of an intellectual disability.

PHYSICAL AND BEHAVIORAL CHARACTERISTICS	Alternative Considerations and Conditions	Recommendations
1. This condition generally is evident in the developmental years; therefore it is sometimes referred to as a "developmental" disability.	**Fetal Alcohol Syndrome/Fetal Alcohol Effect/Maternal Substance Abuse** Children who were premature/preterm at birth often develop more slowly than their chronological age–not catching up until six to nine months of age–or somewhat later.	*Note:* All children benefit from opportunities to interact with children who are different from themselves. The child with cognitive and adaptive dysfunctioning has the opportunity to relate to and observe children whose behaviors and adaptive skills are developmentally appropriate for their age. Through this type of environment, the child can learn important social and adaptive skills.
2. The milestones of early development are usually reached at a later age.		
3. The normal sequences of development are usually not evident.	**Prematurity/Preterm** Children who have English as a Second Language or who come from families of a different culture may have had less opportunity/exposure to everyday activities such as dressing themselves or riding a bike.	All children within an inclusive setting are able to gain acceptance for individual differences and appreciation of each individual's unique skills and strengths.
4. The child finds it difficult to retain information. He/she is often unable to follow simple routines.		
5. Changes in routines and coping with new situations are usually more confusing and upsetting for children with intellectual disabilities.	**Cultural/English as a Second Language/ English with a Dialect** Children who have been in an unstimulating environment with little or no opportunity for exploration or social interaction may function at a below normal developmental level.	*Note:* Be sure that in planning a program for this child that the staff seek ways in which the child can be part of ongoing group activities, and that opportunities for him/her to have positive social experiences with his/her peers are maximized.
6. The child, due to having a short attention span, does not usually stay with most activities for any length of time.		

7. Communication skills are limited. Vocabulary and/or grammar (syntax) are delayed and may be inconsistent in how effectively they are used.

8. Gross and fine motor skills are usually late in developing.

9. The child learns at a much slower rate than other children of his/her age.

10. A lack of age-appropriate self-help/self-care skills is evident.

11. Motivation to learn is generally affected.

12. Rate and retention of learning may be up one day and down the next.

13. The child is often unaware of his/her surroundings and/or fails to explore the environment.

14. The child may have few problem-solving and/or coping skills. He/she does not know how to approach or resolve new activities.

15. Social/emotional behavior is usually delayed.

16. Delay is evident in social/adaptive skills such as sharing and taking turns.

17. The child rarely initiates or contributes new or related ideas to play situations.

18. The child's physical appearance may be different from that of his/her peers.

Note: If the child is prediagnosed as having an intellectual disability, the staff needs to develop a "what to do plan" in order to most effectively include this child in the center.

Speech and Language Problems

Some children, who are age-appropriate in their intellectual development, have problems in language and/or speech.

Cerebral Palsy (mild)

Some children who are above average in height or have birthdays late in the year may appear less advanced when compared with their peer group that is of "average" size and slightly older chronologically.

Children who have been abused or have undergone some emotional trauma may function at a lowered intellectual level.

Abuse/Neglect
Post-Traumatic Stress Disorder

Behavioral/Social/Emotional Problems

Note: In some newly immigrated children, the birth data may be inaccurate.

Children who have had little opportunity to interact with peers and/or little guidance from adults may have delayed social skills.

- Keep an ongoing record of the child's achievements in each area of development (physical, social, cognitive, and emotional).

- In all new activities, plan for repetition and practice.

- Verbal directions/instructions should be consistent and brief.

- Use short sentences with simple vocabulary.

- Demonstrate and frequently repeat any process the child needs to learn.

- Before presenting a new activity, try to have the full attention of the child.

- Use a "task analysis" approach, which is broken down into learning sequential tasks, taking one step of a process at a time until the child has demonstrated that he/she has accomplished that step in the learning sequence. *Do not expect a total sequence to be successfully accomplished at one time.*

- Whenever possible, demonstrate and frequently repeat any process needed to help the child to learn.

- Reinforce successful efforts as soon as they occur, with hugging or verbal approval–for example, "Good job," or name the exact act, "You pounded in that nail really well."

- As often as possible, use multisensory experiences, visual and tactile cues to support oral instructions.

IMPORTANT QUESTIONS TO ASK	Essential Information
1. Are the parents open and willing to let the staff communicate with the agency specialist, teacher, and/or caregiver who has been working with the child? It is important to emphasize that a team approach is needed for successful inclusion of the child.	The center should find out • The name of the agency and the support person who has been working with this child.

• Encourage the child through questions to repeat instructions.

• Provide activities that will help the child to develop his/her fine and gross motor coordination.

• Encourage self-help/self-care skills.

2. Is the center in a position to meet this child's individual needs and continue to meet the needs of the other children in the program? If not, what accommodations and/or additional supports might be considered to enable effective inclusion (volunteer help; high school community programs, and so on)?

• The specific needs of this child—whether there are any physical and/or medical problems; whether he/she has had previous peer experience.

Note: If this child has not had a developmental assessment, this should be recommended to the child's parents. This should be done as soon as possible as it will enable teachers to develop realistic expectations and specific program goals and procedures.

3. What safety and health conditions need to be taken into consideration—for example, does the child need to be carried? How many flights of stairs might this involve? If the child is in a wheelchair, are the door openings in the center wide enough to accommodate the width, and so on.

• Will the specialist be able to come into the center to support and advise staff in programming for the child? If yes, how often?

• Determine the child's strengths, and which areas need the greatest amount of support. Try to use the child's strengths to help overcome his/her weaknesses.

• Is funding available for special equipment/furniture if it is needed?

• Encourage the parents to join a support organization.

4. Are there special program needs? Are they realistic in terms of the staff and the center environment? If not, what additional help can be obtained for the child?

• Is funding available for special staff and/or special training for current staff if the need should arise?

5. Is special equipment/furniture needed and is it readily accessible?

• If the child has additional needs—for example, physical and health challenges, multidimensional programming, with support from a range of specialists may be necessary. Is this available to the center?

6. At what developmental age is the child functioning? Will he/she physically and

Encourage parents to seek help from appropriate specialists such as
• psychologist.
• social worker.
• physiotherapist.
• occupational therapist.
• speech and language pathologist.
• speech and language therapist.
• specialist in children with developmental delays/disorders.

developmentally benefit from the center's group setting? Is he/she toilet trained? Are there facilities for dealing with the child if he/she is not toilet trained?

7. What are the parent's expectations of the center? What are the expectations of the parents for the child? Are they realistic? The help of a psychologist, social worker, and/or community specialist to mediate successful inclusion and determine realistic expectations may be needed.

8. Are the teachers and/or the parents aware of special resources that are available in the community for supporting the inclusion of this child into a group setting of peers?

- Check to see whether the child is eligible for Special Services under the Americans with Disabilities Act (ADA) Title III. In Canada, check Canada's Disability-Childs Benefit.

FRAGILE X SYNDROME

Fragile X syndrome is caused by an abnormality in a specific gene on the X chromosome. This genetic condition is characterized by intellectual disability (mental retardation) and specific physical characteristics.

SPECIFIC CHARACTERISTICS	Important Questions to Ask and Information to Obtain	Treatment/Care/Education
1. It is more common and severe in boys than in girls.	The specific nature of the symptoms varies in each individual child. The center needs to find out the following:	The earlier the child with Fragile X Syndrome is identified, the earlier special care, treatment, and educational goals can be set. It is therefore very important to intervene as early as possible.
2. It may occur in conjunction with other conditions, such as Autism, Prader-Willi Syndrome, Attention Deficit/Hyperactive Disorder.	1. What level of mobility does the child have?	
3. There is no cure for Fragile X Syndrome.	2. Is the child toilet trained?	

PHYSICAL CHARACTERISTICS

Symptoms of Fragile X Syndrome are not present at birth. It is only in later childhood that it becomes physically recognizable. The physical characteristics are more noticeable in boys than in girls.

Characteristics include:

1. large head, long, narrow face, prominent forehead and jaw, large ears.

2. low muscle tone.

3. flexible joints.

4. Strabismus (crossed eyes).

5. high arched palate (in mouth).

6. chest indentation.

7. flat feet.

DEVELOPMENTAL CHARACTERISTICS

1. Though Fragile X is not physically noticeable at birth, one of the first signs is that all developmental milestones are significantly delayed.

2. There are significant delays in cognitive and communication skills.

3. Sensory integration dysfunction is evident.

4. Social, emotional, and behavioral problems are prevalent. Though most children

3. Has the child developed any speech?

4. What other means, if any, has the child of communicating?

5. Does the child have seizures? If yes, how frequently? How are they handled?

6. Does the child have any other medical conditions that the center might have to deal with?

7. Is the child on any medication? If yes, how often does it have to be administered?

8. Has the child any social interaction experience with other children? If yes, explain.

9. Does the child have any special toys or interests? If yes, expand on interests and encourage new uses for the child's favorite toys.

10. Does the child experience any unusual fears and how are these expressed?

11. Does this child tend to be active and/or impulsive? How does the family handle this behavior when it occurs?

Occasionally, a child may enter a child care program exhibiting many of the features associated with Fragile X Syndrome, but has not been formally diagnosed. It may be in the child care program that his/her developmental delays are first recognized. It is extremely important to have the parents take the child to his/her physician for a medical evaluation as soon as any pronounced deviations in development or behavior are noticed.

Because the range of behaviors will vary greatly between children, program goals will also vary. For some program ideas, please see Recommendations in the following sections:

Autism Spectrum Disorder
Attention Deficit/Hyperactive Disorder
Augmentative Communication (under Cerebral Palsy)
Behavioral/Social/Emotional Problems
Curvature of the Spine
Epilepsy
Heart Abnormalities
Intellectual Disabilities
Learning Disabilities (Sensory Integration Dysfunction)
Motor Problems
Speech and Language Problems
Visual Impairment

It is recommended that the child wear a Medic Alert Bracelet.

with Fragile X Syndrome are sociable, they can be shy and anxious in interacting with people they do not know. Tantrums, avoidance of eye contact and stereotypic body movements are all common.

5. Many of these children have attention deficits, hyperactivity, and/or impulsive behavior.

Medical problems that may develop include:

1. sucking problems.

2. digestive disorder–gagging and vomiting.

3. ear and sinus infections.

4. vision problems.

5. curvature of the spine.

6. joint dislocation.

7. heart problems.

8. seizures.

DOWN SYNDROME
(Trisomy 21)

Down Syndrome is a chromosomal disorder caused by an extra 21st chromosome (3 instead of 2). This genetic condition is characterized by specific physical characteristics (noticeable at birth), as well as mild to severe intellectual delays. It affects both male and female children. There is no cure for Down Syndrome.

The center should work closely with any agency or organization that has been working with the child.

If the parents do not have a support group, try to assist them in finding one.

PHYSICAL CHARACTERISTICS

The child may have only a few or many of the following characteristics:

- Floppy limbs
- Short stature
- Overly flexible joints
- Small, round head that appears flattened at the back
- Upward slanted eyes with folds in the corners
- Flat bridged, small nose, often set relatively low in the face
- Protruding tongue because of poor muscle tone, and/or relatively small mouth
- Small, misshapen ears
- Excessive skin at the back of the neck
- Small, wide hands with a deep single (instead of double) crease across one or both palms
- Short fingers and/or toes
- Malformed fifth ("pinkie") finger
- Wide space between the big and second toes
- Unusual creases on soles of feet

BEHAVIORAL/SOCIAL/EMOTIONAL CHARACTERISTICS

- Significant delays in developmental milestones throughout early childhood and adolescence.

- Delays in intellectual development and communication skills will range from mild to significant.

Essential Information

Children with Down Syndrome are prone to getting infections in the respiratory tract—eye, ear, nose, throat, and bronchial tubes. Physicians keep some children with Down Syndrome on antibiotics for extended periods of time.

Approximately half of the children with Down Syndrome have **Heart Abnormalities** and/or intestinal abnormalities.

Early intervention with regard to medical care, treatment, and infant stimulation is extremely important. Many children with Down Syndrome have a peak learning curve when they are younger. Therefore, stimulating games, cognitive, language, and social opportunities are particularly important throughout early childhood.

Important Questions to Ask and Information to Obtain

1. Are there any internal medical conditions of which the center should be aware—heart problems, kidney problems, and so on? Find out in what ways the program may need to be adapted to meet these needs.

Recommendations

Because most children with Down Syndrome are friendly and interactive, it is during the preschool and early school years that basic social interaction skills can be developed.

All young children need to learn limits, sharing, turn-taking, as well as appropriate behavior and voice tone for different environments. It is important that the same basic standards be set for children with Down Syndrome, though in some instances it may take them longer to learn and consistently apply these skills.

Many children with Down Syndrome are affectionate and trusting. It is important to work with the family on helping their child to know when it is and when it is not appropriate to trust adults (e.g., must work on street proofing—especially in urban environments).

For specific programming ideas see the ideas listed under Intellectual Disabilities, as well as those listed under

- **Augmentative Communication** (see **Cerebral Palsy**)
- **Behavioral/Social/Emotional Problems**
- **Epilepsy**
- **Hearing Impairments**
- **Heart Abnormalities**
- **Kidney and Bladder Disorders**
- **Learning Disabilities (Sensory Integration Disfunction)**

- Learning disabilities will range from mild to severe.

- Disposition is generally cheerful and affectionate, facilitating social behavior.

- Able to develop adaptive and early academic skills. The range of future development in these areas varies significantly between different children.

2. Is there any medication that the child must take at regular intervals? If so, find out specifics.

3. Try to obtain a profile of the child's previous experience interacting with other children (siblings, relatives, playmates). This will not only help to estimate his/her level of social interactive skills, but if the child has had only minimal previous interaction, teachers need to anticipate—and help the parents to understand—that there might be an increase in respiratory infections until some immunity is built up.

4. Make sure the child has had flu and pneumonia immunization shots, as well as immunization for all the childhood diseases.

- **Leukemia**
- **Motor Problems**
- **Visual Impairments**
- **Speech and Language Problems**

PRADER-WILLI SYNDROME (PWS)

Prader-Willi Syndrome is a relatively rare genetic birth defect, occurring around the time of conception, and caused by the absence of material on chromosome 15. It is not thought to be an inherited condition. It is found in both sexes and all races, and causes aberrant and inconsistent development. It can be tested for before and after birth.

At birth, children with Prader-Willi Syndrome have very low muscle tone—they are often referred to as "floppy" babies. As infants, they often have to be fed through a tube for a few months because of poor ability to suck due to poor muscle tone. However, by about preschool age, these children begin to eat excessively and gain a great deal of weight.

It is part of the genetic condition—a problem in the hypothalamus—that causes these children to be continuously hungry and never feel that they have eaten enough. No appetite suppressant has been found that works with people with PWS. Therefore, the only solution to controlling weight is an extremely low-calorie diet that must be maintained for all their lives.

Prader-Willi Syndrome usually causes some characteristic facial features and mild to severe intellectual and/or learning disabilities.

SPECIFIC PHYSICAL CHARACTERISTICS/SYMPTOMS	Physical and Emotional Behavior and Essential Information	Recommendations
The physical characteristics of infants and toddlers with Prader-Willi Syndrome are • low muscle tone (hypotonia). • feeding problems (poor sucking ability). • lack of vomit reflex. • excessive sleepiness in infants. • short stature. • small hands and feet. • underdeveloped genitals. • high pain threshold. • delayed motor development or motor problems. • intellectual disabilities (varies from mild to severe). • delayed language development.	The physical behavior of children with PWS is often marked by • temper outbursts. • physical aggression. • stubbornness. • repetitive and often rigid thoughts, verbalizations, and behaviors (obsessive compulsive behavior). • skin picking. All children with PWS • go to great lengths to obtain food. • parents and caregivers may need to lock all access to food when a child with PWS is on the premises, because the gain in weight leads to problems with high blood pressure, respiratory difficulties, diabetes, and so on.	It is believed that with good health care (avoiding weight gain), supportive treatment, and specialized education within a structured environment, most children with Prader-Willi Syndrome will live a normal life span. If a child in the class exhibits a cluster of behaviors related to Prader-Willi Syndrome, the parents should be referred to their child's physician for screening by a medical geneticist. See **Recommendations** under: • **Augmentative Communication Systems** • **Autism Spectrum Disorder** • **Behavioral/Social/Emotional Problems** • **Curvature of the Spine**

- **Diabetes**
- **Heart Abnormalities**
- **Intellectual Disabilities**
- **Learning Disabilities**
- **Motor Problems (Gross and Fine)**
- **Nutritional Deficiencies**
- **Sensory Integration Dysfunction**
- **Speech and Language Problem**s

CRI DU CHAT SYNDROME

Cri du Chat ("cry of the cat") is a rare, severe, genetic disorder. It is caused by a loss or misplacement of genetic material from the 5th chromosome. The absence of this genetic material usually results in abnormal development. It occurs in all races and both sexes.

Most cases of Cri du Chat occur randomly. Very few cases are due to heredity. Blood tests can be performed before or after birth to confirm this syndrome.

PHYSICAL AND BEHAVIORAL CHARACTERISTICS	Essential Information	Recommendations
Children with this condition are usually diagnosed shortly after birth, the first symptom being the high-pitched catlike sound they make when they cry. As well as the catlike crying sound, these children tend to have severe developmental and motor disabilities, including: • poor muscle tone (hypotonia) • small head (microcephaly) • facial features that include wide set eyes, broad nose, low set cars, small jaw, short neck, and so on.	Cri du Chat is a condition that is rare and usually very debilitating. Most children with this condition will have: • intellectual and learning disabilities (moderate to severe). • language problems (receptive language is better than expressive). • delayed motor skills. • self-injurious behavior. • limited self-help skills. • social problems.	If the center has infants and there is a child with delayed development and an unusually whiney, catlike cry, it is important to urge the parents to seek the advice of a medical specialist. This is a condition that is almost always identified in infancy; therefore, if a child with identified Cri du Chat should be enrolled in the center, there should be a number of medical specialists who are already familiar

Medical problems that may develop include:
- recurrent upper respirator tract infections.
- dental problems.
- heart defects.
- poor muscle tone.
- feeding problems.

Note: There is no cure for Cri du Chat. However, with good medical supervision, persons with this condition can live a normal life span.

with the specific strengths, weaknesses, and needs of this child.

See **Recommendations** under:

- **Autism Spectrum Disorder**
- **Augmentative Communication Systems**
- **Behavioral/Social/Emotional Problems**
- **Heart Abnormalities**
- **Intellectual Disabilities**
- **Motor Problems (Gross and Fine)**
- **Nutritional Deficiencies**
- **Sensory Integration Dysfunction**
- **Speech and Language Problems**

Note: Early intervention and appropriate developmental programming can help to ensure a higher quality of life.

RESOURCES

LOCAL

Check for local branches and/or chapters of organizations, associations, societies, institutes, and foundations–many of which are listed under the specific type of intellectual disability (e.g., Down Syndrome).

Parent support groups are also available in many communities.

UNITED STATES

American Association on Mental Retardation
444 North Capital Street NW, Suite 846
Washington, DC 20001-1512
Tel: 1-800-424-3688
Online: http://www.aamr.org

Five Pminus Society (Cri du Chat)
Online: http://www.fivepminus.org

Fragile X Association of Washington State
Online: http://www.wafragilex.org

CANADA

Canadian Association for Community Living
Kinsman Building York University
4700 Keele Street
Toronto, Ontario M3J 1P3
Tel: 1-416-661-9611
Online: http://www.cacl.ca

Canadian Down Syndrome Society
National Office
811-14 Street NW
Calgary, Alberta T2N 2A4
Tel: 1-800-883-5608
Online: http://www.dsat.ca

FRAXA Research Foundation
45 Pleasant Street
Newburyport, MA 01950
Tel: 1-978-462-1866
Online: http://www.fraxa.org

Joseph P. Kennedy Jr. Foundation
1325 G Street
Washington, DC 20005
Tel: 1-202-393-1250
Online: http://www.jpkf.org

National Association for Down Syndrome
P.O. Box 4542
Oak Brook, IL 60522
Tel: 1-630-325-9112
Online: http://www.nads.org

National Down Syndrome Congress
1370 Center Drive, Suite 102
Atlanta, GA 30338
Tel: 1-800-232-6372
Online: http://www.ndsccenter.org

National Fragile X Foundation
P.O. Box 190488
San Francisco, CA 94119-0988
Tel: 1-800-688-8765
Online: http://www.nfxf.org

National Mental Health Association
2001 N. Beauregard Street, 12th Floor
Alexandria, VA 22311
Tel: 1-800-969-6642
Online: http://www.nmha.org

The ARC of the United States Headquarters
1010 Wayne Avenue, Suite 650
Silver Spring, MD 20910
Tel: 1-301-565-3842
Online: http://www.thearc.org

Canadian Mental Health Association
2160 Yonge Street, 3rd Floor
Toronto, Ontario M4S 2Z3
Tel: 1-416-484-7750
Online: http://www.cmha.ca

Internet Mental Health
Online: http://www.mentalhealth.com

Mental Health Web Site
Health Canada
Online: http://www.hc-sc.gc.ca

Ontario Federation of Community Mental Health
    and Addiction Programs
Online: http://www.ofcmhap.on.ca

Ontario Prader-Willi Syndrome Association
1920 Yonge Street, C104
Toronto, Ontario M4S 3E2
Tel: 416-481-8657
Online: http://members.attcanada.ca/~opwsa

Office of Rare Diseases
Online: http://rarediseases.info.nih.gov/ord

Prader-Willi Syndrome Association (USA)
5700 Midnight Pass Road
Sarasota, FL 34242
Tel: 1-800-926-4797
Online: http//www.pwsausa.org

The Association for the Help of Retarded Children
Nassau County Chapter
189 Wheatley Road
Brookville, NY 11545-2699
Tel: 1-516-626-1000
Online: http://www.ahrc.org

ADDITIONAL RESOURCES

KIDNEY AND BLADDER DISORDERS

Kidney and Bladder Disorders affect the functioning of the urinary system. There are many causes of this type of problem, ranging from bacterial infection to physiological abnormalities.

PHYSICAL AND BEHAVIORAL CHARACTERISTICS

The child may experience

1. frequent urination or loss of bladder control, as well as ongoing pain in the area of the kidneys (above the waistline on either side of the child's back).

2. a burning and/or painful sensation when urinating.

3. generalized swelling of the body—eyes, abdomen, feet, or ankles.

4. loss of energy.

5. loss of interest in food.

6. pain in the lower abdomen (bladder infection).

7. fever and/or headaches, and/or pain.

8. puffy eyes upon rising in the morning.

9. only a small amount of urine passed each day; color of urine may be smoky, brown, or red.

10. bed-wetting.

Alternative Considerations and Conditions

Children who are under emotional stress at times regress and lose bladder and/or bowel control.

Some children become so involved in an activity that they forget to go to the bathroom until it is too late.

Heart Abnormalities

Nutritional Deficiencies

Liver dysfunction

Certain types of tumors—especially those in the kidney (Wilms tumor)

Diabetes

It is not uncommon for some children to bed-wet until middle childhood. This is often hereditary. Check to see whether one of the parents, or a parent's sibling, went through a similar pattern.

Delay in maturation of bladder function

Recommendations

- Try to determine whether there are any new changes in the child's life, such as a new baby; a parent who has taken a long trip or left the home; tension between the parents; and/or a death in the family. It is not uncommon for children to regress in a number of areas of development when these types of things are occurring in their lives.

- If the child seems to be forgetting, set up a regular schedule for him/her to go to the bathroom.

- Do not make a big fuss or punish the child if he/she should have an accident.

- Make sure the child is given ample opportunity for intake of liquids and is encouraged to urinate (even if he/she complains that it is painful).

Note: The vast majority of those children who are treated recover completely.

Treatment usually consists of bed rest, specific diet, and appropriate medication.

At times, surgery is required. It is only through a urinalysis that one can determine whether or not the disease is cured.

IMPORTANT QUESTIONS TO ASK THE CHILD'S PARENTS

1. Is this a new pattern of behavior, or have they noticed it on previous occasions (e.g., frequent urination; urinating small amounts each time; complaints from the child of pain, and so on)?

   If the parents have noticed a similar pattern of behavioral change, staff should recommend that they have the child checked by a physician.

2. Are there any new stresses or changes in the child's life?

RESOURCES

LOCAL

Organizations, associations, and kidney foundations supporting persons with kidney dysfunction

Hospital and clinic services

UNITED STATES

National Kidney Foundation Inc.
30 East 33rd Street, Suite 1100
New York, NY 10016
Tel: 1-800-622-9010
Online: http://www.kidney.org

CANADA

Kidney Foundation of Canada
National Office
5165 Sherbrooke Street West, Suite 300
Montreal, Quebec H4A 1T6
Tel: 1-800-361-7494
Online: http://www.kidney.ca

ADDITIONAL RESOURCES

LEAD POISONING

Lead Poisoning is a condition in which lead, which is poisonous at a certain high level of concentration, is absorbed through the skin, swallowed, or inhaled into the body, causing chemical changes in the blood. This may affect many organs and can cause damage to the brain, nerves, red blood cells, and digestive system, resulting in permanent developmental deficiencies.

Children experience more problems than adults do with lead poisoning because of their greater exposure, absorption, and sensitivity to lead. Lead can be stored for many years in the bones, soft tissue, and organs of the young child.

Though the effects of lead poisoning may not be so noticeable during the early years, when the child reaches school age and encounters more demands on his/her ability to learn and concentrate, the damage becomes more obvious.

It should be noted that lead poisoning may occur during the prenatal period.

PHYSICAL CHARACTERISTICS	Alternative Considerations and Conditions	Recommendations
1. If the child has been exposed (prenatally or postnatally) to high levels of lead intake, the child's brain may be damaged during the prenatal stage, as well as after birth, if the child is breast-fed.	Prenatal trauma	• If it is suspected that a child in the center has been exposed to lead poisoning, a simple blood test will reveal whether or not this is true.
2. Because lead may interfere with the amount of calcium absorbed, the teeth, bones, and nervous system of the child may be affected.	Mother's diet during pregnancy Stress	• If lead poisoning is found, make sure that there is an intensive search as to the source of exposure. **Control of Lead in the Environment** In an environment where there is the possibility of lead contamination, the following precautions should be taken with children:
3. Lead often interferes with metabolism (the balance of chemical processes in the body). This may result in abnormal functioning in many of the body systems and in tissue development.	Metabolic dysfunction from other causes	• Wash children's hands frequently and always before eating.
4. Additional physical symptoms that frequently occur are • anemia. • constipation or diarrhea. • nausea, vomiting. • abdominal pain.	Intestinal problems	• Keep children's fingernails clean. • Do not let the children eat food that has dropped on the floor or ground. • Make sure that play areas are away from heavy traffic areas.

- headaches.
- hearing loss.
- fatigue.
- weakness and pain in the joints and muscles.
- pallor.
- loss of appetite.
- sleeplessness.
- seizure disorders.
- coma, even at times death.

LEARNING AND BEHAVIORAL PROBLEMS

Children who have been exposed to an excess of lead intake before or after birth may exhibit the following:

1. Intellectual and/or learning disabilities; not reaching their potential
2. Delays or regression in overall development
3. Poor coordination
4. Slow reaction time
5. Irritability
6. Aggressive behavior disorders
7. Inappropriate social behaviors
8. Speech and language problems
9. Hearing loss
10. Problems in focusing attention
11. Difficulties in the processing of information
12. Learning disabilities
13. Hyperactivity

Arthritis

Environmental influences

Inherited genetic condition, such as Tay-Sachs (degenerative disease)
Intellectual Disabilities
Learning Disabilities
Abuse/Neglect
Brain tumor
Motor Problems
Learning Disabilities (Sensory Integration Dysfunction)
Oppositional Defiant Disorder (ODD)
Behavioral/Social/Emotional Problems
Speech and Language Problems

Hearing Impairment

Attention Deficit/Hyperactive Disorder

Learning Disabilities

- When purchasing painted toys, check to make sure that they are painted with lead-free paint, or that a nontoxic stain or paint has been used. Remove any toys on which the paint has become chipped.
- Watch children who eat nonfood items (pica).
- Have suspected lead-infected soil in the playground area tested.*
- Remove polluted soil and cover the area with grass and wood chips.*
- Make sure that any pipes or walls that are chipping are scraped and repainted with lead-free paint.*

* Have a professional environmental specialist investigate the situation and make repairs.

Known Causes of Lead Poisoning

Transmitters. Lead is transmitted via
- water.
- dust.
- dirt.
- food.

Sources of Lead Poisoning

In Home/School

1. Lead pipes and old-style kettles may cause lead-contaminated drinking water.

2. Lead-based glaze on some dishes presents a hazard.

3. Chipped leaded paint on pipes, walls, and older toys may be swallowed by infants and toddlers.

4. Frequent use of lead-based jewelry, key chains, hairclips, and other personal accessories. (**Note:** Objects high in lead content tend to be heavy for their size, dull gray in color—sometimes painted—and will often leave a gray mark if rubbed against a hard surface.)

5. Hobbies in which lead-based paint is used must be handled with care.

6. Cigarette and fireplace smoke add lead to the air.

7. Scraping, burning, and sanding in renovation of older homes often releases hazardous amounts of lead dust into the air of the room.

8. Parents' occupations sometimes expose children to lead.

9. Certain folk medicines and traditional cosmetics contain large amounts of lead.

Outside of Home

The child may be exposed to

1. contaminated soil or snow.

2. vegetables and fruit grown in polluted soil.

3. car exhaust from lead gasoline.

4. Lead fumes from expressways and gasoline stations that are dangerous if exposure is ongoing (child lives near by).

Note: Today, house paint is almost always lead free, gas is unleaded, and household plumbing is no longer made with lead pipes. However, it is important to be aware that remnants of these hazardous materials may still remain in some environments.

Furthermore, lead does not break down naturally; therefore, it can continue to create problems until it is removed from the environment.

RESOURCES

LOCAL

Health services

Environmental control agencies

UNITED STATES

National Center for Environmental Health
Tel: 1-888-232-6789
Online: http://www.cdc.gov/nceh/lead

National Safety Council
Environmental Health Center
1025 Connecticut Avenue NW, Suite 1200
Washington, DC 20036
Tel: 1-202-293-2270
Online: http://www.nse.org/ehc/lead

The National Lead Information Center
801 Roeder Road, Suite 600
Silver Spring, MD 20910
Tel: 1-800-424-5323
Online: http://www.epa.gov/lead

CANADA

Lead Environmental Awareness and Detection
 (L.E.A.D.)
219 Welland Street
Pembroke, Ontario K8A 5Y5
Tel: 1-613-735-0717
Online: http://www.webhart.net/lead

Health Canada
Tel: 1-800-755-5047
Online: http://www.hc.sc.gc.ca

ADDITIONAL RESOURCES

LEARNING DISABILITIES
(Specific Learning Disorders)

Learning Disabilities encompass problems in which children exhibit disorders in understanding or using spoken and/or written language. They may have problems with listening, processing of information, talking, reading, writing, spelling, and/or mathematics. The child with learning disabilities is deemed to be of average or above average intelligence. Learning disabilities are found in all races, all income levels, and are more common in boys than in girls.

Learning disabilities are often difficult to recognize in young, preschool-aged children. There is evidence of problems in pre-academic skills—for example, acquiring, processing, and retaining information are often very difficult for these children. Frequently, difficulties in gross motor and/or fine motor abilities, problems in visual, auditory, and tactile/kinesthetic perceptions, and/or difficulties in expressive and/or receptive language may be the first evidence of a potential learning disability. It is when the child reaches school age and is expected to learn academic skills such as reading, writing, and mathematics that the specific disabilities become definitively evident.

Dyslexia—problems in reading—including perceiving letters and/or words in reversed direction or upside down, as well as an inability to encode a written word; **Dyscalculia**—a disturbance in the ability to do mathematics; and **Dysgraphia**—problems in the ability to express things in writing—are all terms used to describe specific academic learning disabilities.

PHYSICAL AND BEHAVIORAL CHARACTERISTICS	Alternative Considerations and Conditions	Recommendations

• **Fine and Gross motor skills are generally delayed.**
 	
The child may
 	
1. experience general awkwardness including stumbling easily and problems in activities that require right/left sequencing of feet–such as in climbing, riding a tricycle, and so on.
 	
2. have a fear of heights because of impaired depth perception, evident in behavior on slides, swings, climbing apparatus.
 	
3. have problems in judging when and where a ball will arrive when playing catch, kick ball, and other similar activities.
 	
4. experience general poor sense of directionality–as in finding familiar places.
	Delayed maturation
	
	Intellectual Disabilities
	
	Attention Deficit/Hyperactive Disorder
		• Ask the parents about behaviors and routines at home.
		
		• Keep a developmental record and try to determine the specific areas in which a problem seems to exist.
		
		• Try to provide supports in areas where the child is having difficulty–such as
		   –borders for puzzles
		   –environmental clues/markers to help with directionality
		   –foam balls to use in practicing catching
		   –a trampoline to encourage jumping, and simple obstacle courses that help to practice balance and develop a sense of position in space
		   –paintbrushes with larger handles for grasping
		   –broad markers and crayons

5. be unaware of the direction from which a sound comes.

6. hear sounds louder, interfering with his/her ability to concentrate and/or focus on an activity.

7. have delayed self-help skills such as in dressing, eating, and tying shoes.

8. not have an established hand preference—switches crayon from one hand to the other; eats holding utensil in either right or left hand.

9. have an awkward grasp when holding a crayon, marker, pencil, and/or scissors.

10. have hands that shake or are tense when using writing tools.

11. have poor coordination in coloring, cutting, and pasting activities.

12. have drawings that are developmentally immature.

13. demonstrate an inability to perceive where pieces fit in a puzzle.

14. have poor coordination and perception skills in building activities with blocks and toys that require fitting together and/or linking pieces, and/or placing objects in a specific designated spot.

15. have an inability to build or paint constructively due to poor eye-hand coordination.

Traumatic Brain Injuries

Some children develop right-/left-hand dominance later than others do.

Children who have left-handed dominance may be slowed down if an adult keeps expecting right-handed use—for example, placing objects in the child's right hand or having only right-handed scissors available

Motor Problems

Cerebral Palsy

Late birthday—child may be younger than most others in his/her class because of the birthday month used by the school as a cut-off for this group

Prematurity/Preterm
Lack of opportunities for acquiring these skills

Visual Impairment
Hearing Impairment

Motor Problems

–thicker paper that will not tear if the pressure on it is overly strong.

- Try to break any work or assigned activities into small segments or tasks. Keep directions simple.

- Provide hand-over-hand assistance when needed.

- Have reasonable expectations; do not push the child beyond what he/she is able to do.

- To build the child's self-esteem, give opportunities for the child to achieve in areas where he/she does have strengths.

- Provide opportunities for other children to interact with this child in areas where he/she is able.

- Try to discover and then use the child's strengths to build his/her abilities in areas where he/she is having difficulty.

- In group activities, try to find a role that is suitable to the child's level of functioning that will enable him/her to interact effectively as part of the group.

- Try to build into the daily program some specific activities in which the child can practice needed skills without being withdrawn from the group.

- Use concrete materials in order to present concepts to the different sensory modalities (visual, auditory, and tactile).

16. have an inability to cross the midline when coloring, drawing, eating, or doing puzzles.

17. have confusion between right and left—even after other children have learned this concept.

18. have an inability to follow a sequence of directions—for example, "Please get the pencil and bring it here; then get the paper and scissors."

- **Pre-academic/academic skills** tend to be below expected developmental level.

The child may

1. have uneven patterns of abilities in different areas of development (seem advanced in one area and delayed in another).

2. seem intellectually bright even though his/her performance is very inconsistent in different areas of development.

3. talk later than most children.

4. have spoken language that seems more immature.

5. not ask questions.

6. respond to questions with inappropriate answers.

7. have difficulty in recalling a desired word when speaking—may use associated words such as "dig" for "shovel."

Behavioral/Social/Emotional Problems

Poor teaching or lack of opportunity to learn

Cultural Influences/English as a Second Language/English with a Dialect

Prematurity/Preterm Intellectual Disabilities

There may be feelings of inadequacy from other sources, such as a sibling who teases or parent expectations that are unreasonably high.

The child may be intimidated by his/her peer group, or by a special friend who is more advanced than he/she is.

- Minimize distractions (such as background music; too many bright or interesting objects in front of the child) whenever possible, especially when a new skill is being taught.

- Provide the child with specific learning strategies, perhaps a picture or chart, so that the child can verbalize the necessary procedures to him-/herself.

- Simplify decision-making by restricting the number of choices.

- Limit the number of tasks requested at any one time.

- Design tasks to ensure success and then gradually increase difficulty.

- Provide motivators and incentives, charts, rewards, and praise.

- Make sure work periods are short.

- Seat the child close to the teacher whenever possible in order to monitor his/her work and provide assistance and encouragement.

- Maintain routines, warning the child in advance of changes.

- State rules and expectations clearly. When behavioral consequences are used, they should be consistently applied.

- Focus on recognition of feelings and emotions through the use of puppets and stories.

8. speak too softly or too loudly.

9. have language that is difficult to understand–for example, sequencing and grammar problems.

10. have noticeable problems with processing visual and auditory information despite normal vision and hearing.

11. ignore, confuse, or not follow simple directions or two-step directions or routines.

12. confuse time and space concepts.

13. have problems identifying colors, shapes, numbers, and letters.

14. have difficulty counting in sequence and acquiring number concepts.

15. have trouble with rhyming.

16. have problems with instructional words such as "more," less," "same," "before," "after," and "under."

17. not enjoy looking at books or listening to stories.

18. be unable to tell a simple story in proper sequence.

19. be unable to remember what he has just heard.

20. be unable to locate a named object if the picture is complex.

Family stress factors, such as death, divorce, parent's unemployment, frequent moves, or poor parenting skills.

Hearing Impairment

Cultural Influences/English as a Second Language/English with a Dialect

- Ignore inattention and reinforce on-task behavior.

- Encourage peer interactions with a limited number of children at any one time. Supervise and be firm if the child is hurting another child.

See Suggestions under **Motor Problems**.

Children who have been diagnosed as having **Sensory Integration Dysfunction** (see **Sensory Integration Dysfunction** section) have usually worked with specialists (e.g., occupational therapists).

Staff should have ongoing guidance from a qualified professional who fully understands the specific needs of the child with Sensory Integration Dysfunction and has experience in knowing how to program to meet these needs.

21. have poor academic achievement in spite of average or above average intelligence.

22. have problems in learning the alphabet, number sequence, days of the week, names of colors, shapes, and how to spell and write his/her name.

23. read at a significantly lower level than his/her peers.

24. have difficulty in general acquiring, processing, and retaining information.

25. show a discrepancy between recognition skills and comprehension skills— for example, can read words and/or sentences but does not comprehend what he/she has read.

26. be unable to explain ideas or organize thoughts when relating an experience or making up a story.

27. be very slow in completing written work.

28. have poor printing skills.

29. have trouble with spelling.

30. have trouble with mathematics.

31. have trouble with phonics.

Lack of sleep; physical health problems

Speech and Language Problems
Hearing Impairment
Visual Impairment

Abuse/Neglect

Intellectual Disabilities

Speech and Language Problems

Motor Problems

- **Learning, social, and emotional behaviors** are often immature.

  The child may

  1. not have developed strategies that help one to learn.

  2. be impulsive, make choices quickly—without reflection.

  3. refuse to try, give up easily, and/or expect to fail.

  4. lack motivation in learning activities, appear bored.

  5. be unable to transfer, or have limited transfer of learning to new situations.

  6. not be an independent learner; often seeks adult or peer direction.

  7. have a short attention span.

  8. be distractible; appear to daydream.

  9. forget daily routines, but may remember irrelevant experiences, such as TV commercials.

  10. be overactive; activity seems purposeless.

  11. have frequent changes of mood—for example, overreacts when touched, bumped, or held.

  12. find changes in routine difficult—keeps doing previous activity.

  13. often appear to be unhappy.

Attention Deficit/Hyperactive Disorder

Abuse/Neglect

14. have low self-esteem.

15. appear to be withdrawn or shy, play alone, and seldom talk.

16. engage in disruptive behavior—tantrums, fighting, screaming.

Behavioral/Social/Emotional Problems

17. frequently seek adult attention and approval (may have developed manipulative and avoidance techniques).

18. frequently be in conflict with other children; have few friends.

Oppositional Defiant Disorder

19. prefer to play with younger children.

20. require immediate gratification.

● **Related Social/Emotional Responses**

The child may

Behavioral/Social/Emotional Problems

1. avoid activities that cause him/her problems by actively refusing to try or by showing no interest or motivation to participate.

2. get verbally angry, silly, or emotionally upset when confronted with doing an activity he/she feels unable to manage.

3. be fearful or frightened and withdraw physically and/or emotionally from an activity that makes him/her feel inadequate.

SENSORY INTEGRATION DYSFUNCTION

Sensory Integration Dysfunction is a neurological disorder that can be detected in the early years. It is caused by the brain's inability to integrate information received by the basic sensory systems: *tactile* (touch), *visual* (sight), *auditory* (sound), *olfactory* (smell), *gustatory* (taste), *vestibular* (ability to coordinate the two sides of the body with each other, and the ability to hold one's head upright against gravity), and *proprioceptive* (the ability to move parts of the body in coordination with each other).

The brain's function is to receive sensory messages, process them, and react appropriately. For most children, sensory integration develops well and responses become automatic and appropriate. However, for others, it does not develop properly, and the process of translating input into the brain, and then into an appropriate response, becomes disorganized and inefficient, which results in poor outcomes in development, learning, and behavior.

Sensory integration of the body's basic sensory systems begins before birth and continues throughout life—with the majority of sensory integration occurring before the early teen years.

Note: Each child's sensory integration response system is different—varying in age during the early milestones—ranging from very mild problems to severe dysfunction which continues past the early preschool years.

Neurological disorganization occurs in three different ways:

1. The brain does not receive the message and/or receives it inconsistently (input).
2. The brain receives the message consistently, but does not connect it properly with other incoming sensory messages (processing).
3. The brain does not process all of the sensory messages properly, resulting in inefficient motor, language and/or emotional responses (output).

Sensory Integration Dysfunction can occur in children of all ages, socioeconomic groups, and intellectual levels. More extensive sensory integration dysfunction occurs in children with development disabilities. It is frequently found in conjunction with

- **Intellectual Disabilities (Mental Retardation)**
- **Traumatic Brain Injuries (Brain Trauma)**
- **Cerebral Palsy** and other conditions in which damage to the central nervous system has occurred
- **Premature/Preterm**
- **Autism Spectrum Disorder**
- **Attention Deficit/Hyperactive Disorder**
- **Learning Disabilities**
- **Fetal Alcohol Syndrome, Fetal Alcohol Effect**
- **Down Syndrome**
- **Lead Poisoning**
- **Motor Problems**
- **Behavioral/Social/Emotional Problems**
- **Speech and Language Problems**

Prognosis: If intervention occurs at an early age, Sensory Integration Dysfunction can be managed so that the individual learns how to interact and adapt to his/her environment more effectively.

PHYSICAL AND BEHAVIORAL SYMPTOMS	Recommendations

Note: A child with Sensory Integration problems usually underreacts or overreacts to sensory input, processing, and output.

Some examples of Dysfunctional Sensory Output (that which is observable behavior) **include:**

Tactile (touch)

The child

- avoids physical contact or reacts aggressively when touched.
- avoids messy play—for example, fingerpainting, mud play, wet sand play, and so on.
- dislikes texture of certain materials, toys, or tags on clothing.
- mouths objects.
- does not like wearing clothing and accessories such as hats, gloves, shoes.

Olfactory (smell) and Gustatory (taste)

The child

- cannot stand texture of certain foods, toothpaste, and so on.
- consumes nonedible items such as toothpaste, soap, feces, and so on.
- is a poor/picky eater, with a strong preference for certain foods.
- gets upset/gags at smell of certain food, clothing items, paints, and so on.

Visual (sight) and Auditory (sound)

The child

- is uncomfortable with strong lights/sounds, or seeks sound/light if it is not present.
- covers ears/screams in response to regular "household" noises such as vacuum, flushing toilets, and so on.
- fixates on spinning objects, looking in mirrors, and so on.
- is uncomfortable when the visual environment is rearranged or the environment is changed.
- responds to some sounds and not others—for example, may respond to the sound of a candy wrapper and not to speech.
- does not scan the environment; scans better if objects are moving.

In order to try to successfully include a child with a Sensory Integration Dysfunction in the group, centers will need the support of a specialist—occupational therapist, speech pathologist, behavioral therapist, and/or special education specialist.

A specific program will need to be developed to address the specific needs of the child. At least at the beginning, a child may need full-time one-on-one support as he/she learns the basic routines and requirements of the class and as staff learn specific ways in which to deal with his/her needs.

- Begin by trying to understand what the child's major interests seem to be. If this child is difficult to engage, try to begin with an area or object you think will be of special interest to him/her.

- Some children with Sensory Integration Dysfunction need physical activity—such as bike riding (feeling the wind as well as the coordination of the legs needed for riding); swimming and other water activity that involves buoyancy, and coordination of arms and legs working together; soccer and other games that involve needing to connect a leg or arm with a moving object.

- Activities such as fingerpainting, clay, play dough, planting seeds, and so on, are all areas that involve coordination, as well a sensory exploration, and are often useful for some children with sensory integration dysfunction.

PHYSICAL AND BEHAVIORAL SYMPTOMS	Recommendations
Vestibular (ability to coordinate two sides of the body with each other and hold head upright) The inner ear, besides being used for hearing, provides a sense of balance, and orientation of the body in space. It is this balance that enables us to maintain an upright position.	• It is important for staff to learn as much as they can about Sensory Integration Dysfunction. It is a relatively newly recognized disorder, and there is continually more and more research and insight about it.
The child	
• is fearful of playground equipment, active games, or seeks thrilling fast activities.	• Most children with Sensory Integration Dysfunction have worked with specialists. It is important for the center to obtain (with permission from the parents) recommendations from these specialists—especially if there has been an occupational therapist or someone who can provide ideas for appropriate activities and the most effective placement of the child in a busy room.
• shows no fear, even when fear would be a realistic reaction.	
• experiences car sickness, or extreme dizziness/nausea from any other in-motion activity.	
• is oblivious to heights, moving cars, and so on.	
• spends a lot of time spinning, jumping up and down, and running around.	
• has poor balance—avoids balance activities such as a balance beam.	
Proprioceptive (ability to move parts of the body in coordination with each other) In the body there are internal sensory receptors that coordinate the degree of stretch of muscles and tendons and give the person a sense of balance and awareness of the position of one part of the body to another.	• Most children with Sensory Integration Dysfunction will interact most effectively, whether it is with other people or with toys or projects, if they are in a nondistracting surrounding. This means that the teacher needs to consider how to set up a quiet center in which the child may withdraw in order to work most effectively.
The child:	
• will apply too much or too little pressure when handling toys or touching people.	
• enjoys deep massage, scratching of his/her back, but may be scared of light touch.	
• has either low or high pain and/or temperature threshold.	
• involves him-/herself in excessive hair pulling, biting, hitting of walls and/or objects, head banging, and other self-injuries.	
• fatigues easily or becomes overactive.	
• finds it difficult to maintain a sitting position for very long.	
• has poor motor planning skills—is clumsy.	
• leans on furniture or walls to maintain stability/balance.	

PHYSICAL AND BEHAVIORAL SYMPTOMS	Recommendations

Complex Activities and Sensory Integration Dysfunction

As the child develops, the lack of integration of one or more of the basic sensory systems interferes with more complex activities such as learning and social/emotional development.

The child may

- have poor learning-how-to-learn skills–organization, scanning, and the like.

- be impulsive, be careless, lack control, be aggressive, and/or have temper tantrums.

- find it difficult to relax/calm down.

- be careless, be sloppy in appearance, and/or have poor self-care skills.

- have difficulty with transition times.

- have poor self-esteemand/or few friends.

- have delays in motor skills (gross and fine), speech and language, as well as academics.

Children with the following conditions frequently show signs of concurrent Sensory Integration Dysfunction:

(in alphabetical order)

- **Autism Spectrum Disorder**
- **Attention Deficit Disorder**
- **Cerebral Palsy** and other conditions in which damage to the central nervous system has occurred
- **Fetal Alcohol Syndrome/Fetal Alcohol Effect** and other Substance Abuse
- **Intellectual Disabilities**
- **Prematurity (Preterm)**
- **Traumatic Brain Injury**

See related sections for recommendations.
Seek guidance from an occupational therapist.

If a child has not been diagnosed as having Sensory Integration Dysfunction during the preschool years, but appears to have some developmental delays, see the following sections for useful recommendations:

- **Visual Impairment**
- **Hearing Impairment**
- **Motor Problems (Gross and Fine)**
- **Speech and Language Problems**

RESOURCES

LOCAL

Local hospitals, clinics, and other agencies that provide developmental assessments and services for children with learning disabilities

Physicians (for the purpose of referral for evaluation and to rule out other types of problems)

Early childhood development specialists (clinics, colleges and universities, local boards of education, and so on)

UNITED STATES

Council for Exceptional Children
110 North Glebe Road, Suite 300
Arlington, VA 22201
Tel: 1-703-620-3660
Online: http://www.cec.sped.org

Learning Disabilities Association of America
4156 Library Road
Pittsburgh, PA 15234-1349
Tel: 1-412-341-1515
Online: http://www.ldanatl.org

National Center for Learning Disabilities
381 Park Avenue South, Suite 1401
New York, NY 10016
Tel: 1-888-575-7373
Online: http://www.ncld.org

Sensory Integration Resource Center
S.I. network
Online: http://www.sinetwork.org

Sensory Integration International
The Ayers Clinic
P.O. Box 5339
Torrance, CA 90510-5339
Tel: 1-30-787-8805
Online: http://www.sensoryint.com

CANADA

Canadian Dyslexia Association
290 Picton Avenue
Ottawa, Ontario K1Z 8P8
Tel: 1-613-722-2699
Online: http://www.dyslexiaassociation.ca

ADDITIONAL RESOURCES

LEUKEMIA

Leukemia is essentially a form of cancer in which there is an uncontrolled proliferation of abnormal white blood cells that spread into the bloodstream where they multiply and spread into other organs, attacking the tissue in the bone marrow, spleen, and/or lymph nodes. The most frequent symptoms are enlarged lymph nodes, liver, and spleen.

Leukemia is the most common form of childhood cancer and occurs more frequently in boys. Most children treated medically for leukemia make a full recovery.

PHYSICAL AND BEHAVIORAL CHARACTERISTICS	Alternative Considerations and Conditions	Recommendations
The child may be experiencing 1. tiredness. 2. paleness of the skin. 3. aches and pains in his/her joints and bones. 4. excessive bruising. 5. small burst blood vessels on the skin. 6. excessive bleeding from the gums. 7. swollen glands (swelling in the neck, armpits, and groin due to enlarged lymph nodes). 8. fever and/or night sweating. 9. weight loss/failure to gain weight. 10. sleeplessness. 11. susceptibility to infections. *Note:* There are additional symptoms that are more medical in nature and are not observable by the layperson.	Iron deficiency Anemia **Arthritis** **Abuse/Neglect** **Hemophilia** (and other blood clotting problems) **Allergies** Tumors Hodgkin's disease (malignancy) Drug reaction **Failure to Thrive** (nonorganic) The child may have a routine at home that does not allow for enough sleep. The child may have an inappropriate diet.	• If staff notice increased bruising and tiredness in a child, share your observations with the parents and recommend that the child have a complete medical checkup. **If a child comes to the center pre-diagnosed with leukemia**, the following recommendations should be taken into consideration. • The child should be treated as normally as possible. • It is important to get a physician's recommendations in writing. • The taking of medication should become a nonemphasized part of the child's routine at the center. • If the child needs rest periods or "time out" from excessive exertion, this should be accepted with as little ado as possible. • Record any evidence of bruising and/or excessive tiredness and/or complaints of aches and pains. • Be sure to include the date, time of day, and the specifics of the complaint or

Children may come to your center pre-diagnosed.

IMPORTANT QUESTIONS TO ASK

1. Will the child need to take pills or other medication at school? Is the child able to do this on his/her own or is supervision needed?

2. Are there any side effects to the medication the child is taking? If yes, what are they?

3. For which childhood and other diseases has the child been immunized?

4. Are there any precautions the center needs to take in order to avoid infections?

5. Has the child spent time in the hospital? If yes, note the age at which this occurred, for how long it occurred, and so on.

6. Is the child currently undergoing any treatment? How often? In-patient or outpatient?

Note: It is important to impress on the parents the importance of their keeping in touch with the center and advising the staff with regard to any treatment or hospitalization their child might have to experience.

Essential Information

If the child is on medication, it is important to know the level of responsibility that the center must take—any special storage conditions, and so on.

Certain medications cause mood changes; therefore, it is useful to know whether this occurs in this child.

Some forms of treatment for leukemia result in a temporary loss of hair on the child's head.

Because children with leukemia usually have a reduced immune system (often because of the medication they are on), the family will need to know within 72 hours if the child has been exposed to any contagious diseases. This allows the family to take preventative measures.

observation. Observation should be initialed by the teacher so that if details are needed, it is easy to find the observer.

- Basically, this child will need limits and support and help in building social skills as much as, and possibly more than, other children. This is because
  - the child may have been in isolation in the hospital.
  - the child may have had few opportunities for play, because the parents have limited contact with other children, fearing their child will catch infections and become ill if he/she plays with other children.
  - the child's parents may have been overprotective and/or oversolicitous, because of the child's ill health and susceptibility to infections.

- Families of other children need to know how important it is to let the center know if their child contracts an infectious disease.

- Ongoing contact with the family and the child's physician is extremely important. The center needs to have a clear picture of any limitations or recommendations that will support the child.

- The parents of a child with leukemia will probably need extra reassurance and support as they experience ongoing emotional ups and downs as their child goes through periods of medical treatment and recuperation.

- It is also important that other children in the center be prepared ahead of time if the child is likely to lose his/her hair. Explain that sometimes when people get sick, in order to make them well again, they have to take special treatment that may make their hair fall out; that the hair will grow back but that during the time that the child has a loss of hair, the child needs to be accepted as he/she is. The teacher is a model for demonstrating this acceptance.

RESOURCES

LOCAL

Leukemia associations, organizations, and so on

Cancer societies, associations, and organizations

Hospital/clinic services for cancer and blood disorders

UNITED STATES

American Cancer Society
Tel: 1-800-227-2345
Online: http://www.cancer.org

National Cancer Institute
6116 Executive Boulevard, MSC 8322
Suite 3036A
Bethesda, MD 20892-8322
Tel: 1-800-422-6237
Online: http://www.cancer.gov/cancer

The Leukemia and Lymphoma Society
1311 Mamaroneck Avenue
White Plains, NY 10605
Tel: 1-914-949-5213
Online: http://www.leukemia.org

CANADA

Canadian Cancer Society
National Headquarters
10 Alcorn Avenue, Suite 200
Toronto, Ontario M4V 3B1
Tel: 1-416-961-7223
Online: http://www.cancer.ca

Health Canada
Health Protection Branch
ALO900C2
Ottawa, Ontario K1A 0K9
Tel: 1-613-957-2991
Online: http://www.hc-sc.gc.ca

Leukemia Research Fund of Canada
Tel: 1-800-668-8326
Online: http://www.leukemia.ca

ADDITIONAL RESOURCES

MOTOR PROBLEMS (Gross and Fine)

Motor/Coordination Problems refers to children who are experiencing delays in the development of gross and/or fine motor coordination. The child's motor functioning level is below the expected developmental level for a child at his/her given age and intellectual level.

These developmental motor/coordination problems should not be associated with specific medical conditions such as cerebral palsy or muscular dystrophy, though many of the program recommendations and considerations are suitable for children with any type of motor/coordination problem.

GROSS MOTOR

PHYSICAL CHARACTERISTICS	Alternative Considerations and Conditions	Recommendations
Think in terms of the expected developmental level for a child at a given age and intellectual level. The child may 1. appear clumsy, run awkwardly, trip over his/her own feet, and/or be a slow runner. 2. be unable to walk up or down stairs or climb a ladder using alternating feet. 3. walk with a wide-based gait. 4. have balance that appears awkward, stays close to the wall. 5. be unable to climb up/down a jungle gym. 6. have difficulty jumping and/or hopping, galloping, skipping, and/or standing on one foot. 7. be unable to bounce, catch, and/or toss large balls or bean bags. 8. have difficulty in getting up to a standing or sitting position.	**Visual Impairment** Visual/motor problem Tonal (large muscle) problem Neurological problem Feet that are pigeon-toed or point outwards Inner ear infection causing balance problem **Sensory Integration Dysfunction** **Hearing Impairment** Poorly fitting shoes There may have been little previous experience in gross motor play if child has few peers or adults to interact with in active play, or if play space is limited.	• Keep a developmental record and try to determine the specific nature of the problem. • Check the child's medical history for any sign of birth injury. • If questions remain, recommend that the child have a full medical assessment. • Try to build into the daily program some specific activities in which the child can practice needed skills. **Specific activities to support gross motor development:** • Trampolines or mattresses and/or balancing beams for jumping and balancing • Obstacle courses, using large blocks, pillows, chalk lines, or rope lines on the floor to create a track • Felt or cardboard shapes set up in different patterns on the floor for crawling, walking, hopping, and jumping

9. have problems in rolling over from front to back or vice versa.

10. have poor skills in motor planning–bike riding, skating, and so on.

11. not alternate arms and legs appropriately when walking or running.

12. have difficulty with sitting balance (slumps over; in young children may have head on table).

13. constantly shift position on a chair due to balance problems.

14. fatigue easily.

15. seem accident prone, bumps into furniture, people, or other objects.

Nutritional Deficiencies

Cerebral Palsy (mild)

Autism Spectrum Disorder
Sensory Integration Dysfunction

Abuse/Neglect

Anemic (iron deficiency)
Lead Poisoning
Heart Abnormalities
Curvature of the Spine

- Games such as Twister or Statues for the child to hold awkward positions (positions can vary in degree of difficulty)

- Games such as Simon Says or This is the Way We … that demand imitative, easy-to-do motions

FINE MOTOR

BEHAVIORAL CHARACTERISTICS	Alternative Considerations and Conditions	Recommendations

The child may have an

1. immature hand/finger grip (weak grasp or over grasp, leading to dropping objects).

2. inability to manipulate effectively tools like eating utensils and scissors.

3. inability to pick up small objects (poorly developed pincer grasp), such as puzzle pieces and beads.

4. inability to place objects in balanced relation to one another, such as building

Some children develop right-/left-hand dominance later than others do. This may influence fine motor skills

Children who have left-hand dominance may be slowed down if an adult keeps expecting right-handed use, for example, placing objects in the child's right hand; having only right-handed scissors available.
Learning Disabilities
Sensory Integration Dysfunction

Specific activities to support fine motor development:

- Observe the child for handedness and expose him/her to more fine motor experiences.

- Modeling clay, play dough, fingerpaints, and other manipulative materials.

- finger plays.

- painting, chalking, crayoning.

- buttoning, zippering.

a tower of blocks, putting pegs in a pegboard, bead stringing.

5. inability to draw with form–unable to manipulate writing tools effectively.
   - holds pencil/crayon too high or too low.
   - arm is in the air instead of on the table when drawing, coloring, or painting.

6. inability to cross midline when coloring, drawing, eating, or doing puzzles.

7. inability to effectively carry out tasks that require specific turning and manipulating, such as turning doorknobs, unscrewing lids, buttoning, zippering, and so on.

8. inability to draw simple geometric shapes and pictures.

9. inability to print large and small letters and/or numerals.

The child may

1. avoid activities that cause him/her problems by actively refusing to try or showing no interest or motivation to participate.

2. do a messy, sloppy, or slipshod job, scribbling over fine motor work, just to get it over with.

Poor dexterity may be related to
- overall muscle weakness
- poorly developed individual finger muscles
- lack of previous opportunity to practice these skills.

Visual Impairment

There may be poor depth perception (an inability to see or place objects in desired relationship to each other).

There may be a lack of voluntary control to release objects.

Learning Disabilities
Cerebral Palsy (mild)
Muscular Dystrophy
Autism Spectrum Disorder
Abuse/Neglect

Abuse/Neglect

There may be feelings of inadequacy from other sources, such as a sibling who teases or parent expectations that are unreasonably high.

Specific activities to support visual perceptual motor development:
- Placing articles in relation to one another
- Making collages (range of shapes and textures)
- Wood gluing
- Using form boards
- Building with blocks
- Using small fit-together blocks
- Beading-imitating patterns with beads, pegs, and so on
- Stacking toys in progressive size order
- Pouring from one container to another
- Buttoning, bolting, locking
- Hammering and nailing

Specific activities to support wrist/hand manipulating:
- Turning knobs
- Unscrewing lids
- Buttoning, zippering, and so on

Specific activities to support hand strength and grasp:
- Clay, play dough, punching, pulling, and so on
- Papier-mâché
- Squeezing activities–wringing wet cloths, sponges, games where squeezing results in a sound

3. have no pride in anything he/she makes; be unwilling to take work home or share it with others.

4. get verbally angry, silly, or upset when confronted with doing an activity he/she cannot manage.

5. be fearful or frightened and withdraw physically or emotionally from an activity that makes him/her feel inadequate.

The child may be intimidated by his/her peer group, or by a special friend who is more advanced than he/she is.

Behavioral/Social/Emotional Problems

The child may have a low threshold for frustration or feelings of failure and withdraw rather than attempt to develop and practice a skill.

Dramatic centers with opportunities to develop fine motor skills include:

- post office (mail sorting).
- store (handling products and money).
- tea party (pouring, baking).
- cooking activities, such as cutting cookies, peeling apples or carrots, and pouring ingredients.

Note: Try to alter situations to meet specific needs—for example, provide left-handed scissors (or be sure the scissors work for both hands), pencil/crayon grips, position paper correctly, and monitor seating for left-handed children.

In general, remember to:

- try to avoid competitive situations that make the child feel more inadequate.
- provide as much verbal, visual, and physical support as possible to help the child. At the same time, do not separate him/her from his/her peer group.
- try to provide activities that are fun and that will help the child develop feelings of success (no right or wrong outcome), such as fingerpainting, cookie decorating, washing doll clothes, and so on.

Note: Be sure to notice and express pleasure to the child when a new skill is achieved.

Note: If no improvement is observed after following these recommendations, or if the motor concerns are still evident as the child approaches the age at which written skills are expected, recommend to the parents that they have the child assessed by an occupational therapist or special education consultant.

RESOURCES

LOCAL

Local hospitals, clinics, and other agencies that provide developmental assessments

Physicians (for the purpose of determining specific problem, if more pervasive than developmental)

Early childhood development specialist (clinics, colleges and universities, local boards of education, and so on)

UNITED STATES

American Occupational Therapy Association (AOTA)
4720 Montgomery Lane
P.O. Box 31220
Bethesda, MD 20824-1220
Tel: 1-800-668-8255
Online: http://www.aota.org

CANADA

Canadian Association of Occupational Therapists (CAOT)
CTTC Building, Suite 3400
1125 Colonel By Drive
Ottawa, Ontario K1S 5R1
Tel: 1-800-434-2268
Online: http://www.caot.ca

ADDITIONAL RESOURCES

MUSCULAR DYSTROPHY

Muscular Dystrophy is a genetic condition in which there is a progressive weakening and wasting away of certain muscles in the body, resulting in a progressive loss of muscular control. As muscle tissues waste away, fatty and connective tissue replace them.

Muscular dystrophy can be passed on by the parents or can be caused by a genetic mutation and therefore may occur spontaneously in a single individual. It is caused by a dysfunction in a specific gene that is associated with muscle functioning.

There is no known cure and no way to permanently arrest the progression of the disease.

There are five major types of muscular dystrophy, their classifications being based on the groups of muscles primarily involved, the age of the onset, or change in muscle tone and reactivity of the muscles. The most frequent type is Duchenne. This is found mostly in boys and develops in children between the ages of two and six years. It is usually passed on genetically through the mother who carries the gene but does not have muscular dystrophy.

Most other dystrophies have a later age of onset.

SPECIFIC CONSIDERATIONS	Essential Information	Recommendations
If a child has been prediagnosed as having muscular dystrophy, then it is important to have contact with the agency and/or doctor working with the family. Find out what, if any, limitations there will be on the child's activity.	In accommodating this child in the center, consider how 1. many flights of stairs must be climbed. 2. to provide adequate support and supervision during gym and outdoor play activities.	• Based on information obtained, the center has to decide on the best way to accommodate this child. If it does not seem possible because of the physical layout, it is important to find out alternatives to recommend to the parents. • Exercise and activity will not hurt this child. The child should be encouraged to participate in as many activities as possible.
IMPORTANT QUESTIONS TO ASK 1. What is the extent of his/her mobility? Is the child in a walker, wheelchair, calipers, or braces? 2. What is the extent of his/her immobility? To what extent is his/her coordination affected?	• It is important to work with support agencies and find ways to most effectively help the family and the child to cope with the progressive degeneration of physical ability.	• Be aware that a child may be self-conscious about his/her progressively worsening motor skills (particularly if the child is aware that he/she is falling further and further behind as his/her peers gain new abilities). Do not press the child into situations that will expose his/her limitations, possibly increasing the child's self-consciousness.

3. Is the child toilet trained? What is the toileting routine?

4. Does the child have any other health problems associated with the muscular dystrophy?

5. Is the child on any medication?

If the child has not been previously diagnosed and Muscular Dystrophy is suspected, symptoms to look for include:

1. regression in gross motor development. The child begins to waddle, has difficulty climbing stairs, falls more easily, or has trouble picking him/herself up from a fall.

2. when trying to stand from a sitting position, the child pushes, walking up legs with his/her hands, in order to stand.

3. calf muscles in the legs that may appear enlarged. This is caused by fatty deposits and is often misinterpreted as muscle tissue.

4. muscles in the limbs and trunk that appear wasted.

5. frequent trips and falls.

6. inability to jump or hop normally.

7. tendency to walk on tiptoes.

8. mild learning disabilities.

Alternative Considerations and Conditions

Behavioral/Social/Emotional Problems

Imitating younger sibling in the family who is receiving a lot of attention as he/she begins to walk

Nutritional Deficiencies
Learning Disabilities (Sensory Integration Dysfunction)
Poor sense of balance
Motor Problems
Learning Disabilities
Autism Spectrum Disorder

- Check with the child's parents for any family history or indication of other possible causes for weakness of muscle tone.

- If the parents express concern, or if the child has not been diagnosed, refer the child to his physician for a complete medical examination.

- Physiotherapists can work with the child and teach the parents/caregivers certain therapeutic techniques that can be used to help maintain the child's muscular strength, and use posture that will help the child to maximize his/her strength.

  Note: There are physical exercises of stretching weakened muscles that can help to delay some of the deformities that might occur more quickly without this type of daily regime.

- An individual exercise program must be established for the child. A physiotherapist is usually the person who determines the child's specific needs.

RESOURCES

LOCAL

Muscular dystrophy associations, organizations, societies. Look for local chapter in your city or town.

Hospital/clinic and support services.

Doctors who specialize in neurology, geneticists, physiotherapists, and occupational therapists can all provide information that supports families dealing with a child with muscular dystrophy.

UNITED STATES

Muscular Dystrophy Association–USA
National Headquarters
3300 E. Sunrise Drive
Tucson, AZ 85718
Tel: 1-800-572-1717
Online: http://www.mdausa.org

CANADA

Muscular Dystrophy Association of Canada
Regional Office
2345 Yonge Street, Suite 901
Toronto, Ontario M4P 2E5
Tel: 1-800-567-2873
Online: http://www.mdac.ca

ADDITIONAL RESOURCES

NUTRITIONAL DEFICIENCIES

Nutritional Deficiencies occur when the body lacks one or more essential elements (e.g., vitamins, minerals) obtained from food, and/or a general deficiency of calories.

PHYSICAL CHARACTERISTICS	Alternative Considerations and Conditions	Recommendations
The child may have 1. a pale complexion; skin that looks dull/rough. 2. a body build/structure that deviates from the norm (bulging, bloated stomach; rib cage that protrudes; legs that are badly bowed). 3. poor posture, poor muscle tone, and/or poor coordination. 4. poor or no appetite. 5. an increasing loss of energy; lethargic reactions. 6. frequent illness and infection. 7. frequent constipation, diarrhea, or nausea. 8. upper respiratory infections, wheezing, stuffiness of the nose, sneezing, or eyes that look red or infected. 9. loss of weight. 10. growth delay. 11. poor absorption of food in small intestines resulting in bowel problems. ***Note:*** Nutritional deficits may be noted during a growth spurt period when nutritional needs increase.	Previous conditions of extreme deprivation, such as having been in a refugee camp with minimal resources Inherited (genetic) Lack of exercise Problem with muscle development Swollen adenoids (cannot smell; no sense of taste) Reaction to medication Stomach disorder Digestive tract disorder Gastrointestinal problems Parental attitudes about food Tension/stress/lack of sleep Exposure to illness at home Chronic illness, infection or lack of immunity **Asthma** **Allergies** **Leukemia** **Diabetes**	• Try to find out from the parents if there is a physical reason for the child's condition. • If the center is unable to obtain useful information from the parents, recommend that the child's physician be consulted with respect to having the child evaluated. • An up-to-date multicultural food guide for young children should be posted and discussed with the parents. Remember that the center acts as a model. It is important to prepare (where applicable) nutritious food, as well as, to encourage the parents to • provide nutritional snacks (cheese, fruit, vegetables). • include nutritious foods in dishes that the child likes (sauces, puddings, casseroles); try different methods of food preparation. • serve the child small amounts of each type of food. • encourage the child to taste everything, but do not force or bribe. • avoid too many snacks and excessive fluids between meals.

BEHAVIORAL CHARACTERISTICS

The child may

1. refuse to eat; be a selective, picky eater; or have a depressed appetite.

2. have pica–craving to eat nonfood substances such as soil, chalk, and so on.

3. have a short attention span.

4. be anxious.

5. have hyperactive/hypoactive behavior.

6. lack motivation, or have poor self-concept.

7. be sluggish or withdrawn, sleepy or irritable.

8. have poor visual/motor coordination.

9. be frequently absent from school.

The child may have inexperience with certain foods, or a different time pattern for eating meals.

Cultural/English as a Second Language/ English with a Dialect
Autism Spectrum Disorder

Attention Deficit/Hyperactive Disorder
Learning Disabilities
Abuse/Neglect

Metabolic imbalance

Family-imposed dietary restrictions that lead to deficits in the child's diet (e.g., an improperly balanced vegetarian diet)

Abuse/Neglect

- avoid distractions such as toys on the table or having the television on during meal times.

- not persist in offering rejected foods–wait for a week or two before introducing them again.

- not punish or reward the child for eating. For instance, do not withhold dessert until he/she finishes a particular dish.

- make eating time relaxed and happy. Talk about what the children have done that day, plans for the rest of the day or the next day, things they have been doing at home, and so on.

- encourage participation in noncompetitive games and physical activities that do not demand a great amount of physical energy.

- help the child extend the amount of time he/she spends at an activity (including meal time)–conversing, counting, and discussing color, texture, and other aspects of the activity or food.

Note: It is important to maintain an ongoing dialogue with the parents. If the parents are non-English speaking/reading, you might try to obtain some nutritional information in their home language.

RESOURCES

LOCAL

Hospital dietitians and nutritionists will often offer support and printed material.

Check for health officials, nurses, and other community and agency specialists in your area.

UNITED STATES

American Dietetic Association Headquarters
216 Jackson Boulevard
Chicago, IL 60606-6995
Tel: 1-312-899-0040
Online: http://www.eatright.org

American Society for Nutritional Sciences
9650 Rockville Pike, Suite 4500
Bethesda, MD 20814-3998
Tel: 1-301-530-7110
Online: http://www.asns.org

Food and Nutrition Information Center
10301 Baltimore Boulevard
Beltsville, MD 20705-2351
Tel: 1-301-504-5719
Online: http://www.nalusda.gov/fnic

CANADA

Dietitians of Canada
480 University Avenue, Suite 604
Toronto, Ontario M5G 1V2
Tel: 1-416-596-0857
Online: http://www.dietitians.ca

Health Canada
Food and Nutrition Headquarters
A.L. 0900 C2
Ottawa, Ontario K1A 0K9
Tel: 1-613-957-2991
Online: http://www.hc-sc.gc.ca

National Institute of Nutrition
265 Carling Avenue, Suite 302
Ottawa, Ontario K1S 2E1
Tel: 1-613-235-3355
Online: http://www.nin.ca

ADDITIONAL RESOURCES

POST-TRAUMATIC STRESS DISORDER (PTSD)

Post-Traumatic Stress Disorder (PTSD) is a condition found in children and adults that results from exposure (personal or second hand) to an extreme traumatic event. It should be noted that some people develop PTSD and others do not—or they may develop symptoms months or years later.

Stressors may include:
- natural disasters such as floods, fires, tornados.
- accidents—such as car accidents, being burned or seeing someone burned, and/or falling from a high place.
- war—whether experienced personally or seen on television.
- witnessing death or experiencing a brutal death of a friend or family member.
- civilian or urban violence—such as witnessing a murder, someone being brutally beaten, other street crimes, or someone breaking into the child's house.
- severe physical or psychological illness, either experienced by oneself or observing it in someone with whom one is emotionally and/or physically attached or bonded.
- family violence, including any behaviors that the child witnesses and/or perceives as threatening to him-/herself or those he/she loves; family and/or individual trauma, including physical and/or sexual abuse.
- maltreatment, neglect, inconsistent caring on the part of those who the child perceives as the important people in his/her life.

The child may or may not realize at the time the incident occurs that he/she has experienced trauma (e.g., one-time exposure or repeated events such as in sexual abuse). The symptoms of distress and feelings of fear must last for at least a month for the condition to be classified as PTSD.

PHYSICAL AND EMOTIONAL BEHAVIORS	Alternative Considerations and Conditions	Recommendations
The child may experience 1. feelings of helplessness, anxiety, fear, lack of control, and/or panic attacks in tension-producing situations. 2. upsetting memories or thoughts of the traumatic experience (flashbacks). 3. unexpressed fears triggered by reminders of the event. These may result in avoidance behaviors such as refusing to talk or to go near a certain area or person.	**Behavioral/Social/Emotional Problems** **Abuse/Neglect**	• If the child has experienced a traumatic incident, it is important to allow him/her to play out the incident, as well as any themes that relate to it. The teacher should be accepting, supportive, and non-judgmental. • Many children benefit from drawing/painting pictures about their trauma. • Try to provide consistency—routines that will make the child feel secure and safe.

4. anxiety and depression (may suddenly become clingy and afraid of leaving parents; fear of new situations, and so on).

5. and/or develop regressive behaviors—such as losing bladder and/or bowel control, crying more frequently, and so on.

6. memory, concentration, and attentiveness problems.

7. loss of interest in activities that he/she previously enjoyed.

8. disorganized and/or agitated behavior.

9. aggressive behavior that was not previously evident.

10. an inability to relax.

11. mood changes.

12. increased sensitivity to sounds (often startle reactions) from sirens, planes, horns honking, thunder, and so on.

13. sleeplessness and/or difficulty falling asleep; and/or recurrent, stressful dreams, such as nightmares. These may or may not be about the original incident.

14. changes in sleeping and/or eating patterns.

15. nausea, rapid heartbeat, muscle tension, and/or diarrhea.

16. outbursts of anger.

17. worries about violence.

18. self-abusive behavior.

Attention Deficit/Hyperactive Disorder

Behavioral/Social/Emotional/ Problems

Essential Information

- Most children who are exposed to trauma do not develop PTSD. Children who do develop PTSD usually do this within the first weeks or month (though it can occur years) after the event.

- It is important to realize that the child may not react immediately to a traumatic event. Or he/she may react and then seem to stop, only to begin to show symptoms of PTSD one to three months later.

- If the parents, teachers, or important people in the child's life are experiencing a great deal of stress or distress, and are not able to handle their feelings and emotions, this will almost always have a negative impact on the child.

- If the whole family has undergone a traumatic experience—such as a fire that has burned out their house; a death in the family; physical harm being done to a

Note: If the child seems to be only able to play and/or draw the traumatic incident and to do it over and over again, it is recommended that the family have the child assessed and supported by a trained specialist.

- Try to avoid situations that create constant reminders of the traumatic incident. At the same time, if an incident occurs that triggers anxiety in the child, be reassuring and help the child to understand that in this instance he/she does not need to be scared because, for example, there are many people around, the teachers are there to watch him/her, and so on.

- Some children need to talk about what happened to them. It is important to be a nonjudgmental listener. If you do not want other children to hear what the child has to say, go with the child to an area in which he/she can talk and in which reflective and supportive responses can be given by the teacher.

Note: **Do not try to play therapist.** If a child's symptoms are increasing and he/she is experiencing increasing stress, or has shown no improvement for over three months, it is important to get the family in touch with a specialist who can work with the child and family. A qualified play therapist is often helpful in supporting young children in working through situations.

19. physical ailments—abdominal pains, headaches, stomach aches, and so on— that seem to have no physiological basis.

20. avoidance of activities associated with the trauma/incident.

family member; and so on–it is extremely important that the family receive support from people and groups in their community.

SOCIAL BEHAVIORS

The child may

1. experience difficulty in playing with other children, fighting, and not being able to play cooperatively when prior to the traumatic incident there were no problems in this area.

2. become stubborn, defiant, and/or negative in response to simple requests.

3. not be able to express in words what he/she is experiencing because of limited language development.

4. become withdrawn; act out sexually and/or aggressively—depending on the nature of the trauma.

5. have difficulty maintaining friendships.

Important Questions to Ask

1. What was the nature of the extreme traumatic situation that occurred?

2. When did the incident occur?

3. What behavior changes have the parents noticed since the incident occurred?

4. Have the parents noted any new fears that the child is experiencing?

5. Have the parents noticed any changes in the child's play and/or drawings? Does the child seem to be replaying the incident in his/her play and/or artwork?

6. Is the child showing signs of being aware of the sight in which the trauma occurred. How does he/she react?

7. Is the child receiving any psychological help–for example, play therapy? If yes, can the center talk with the therapist in order to get support in how to most effectively work with the child?

8. Is the child on any medication for anxiety, sleeplessness, and so on?

9. Is the family receiving any help in dealing with the problem–family therapy?

RESOURCES

LOCAL

In some areas, hospitals/clinics have outpatient services for children who have experienced trauma.

Crisis centers for adults may provide services for children and/or may have suggestions for referral.

UNITED STATES

Anxiety Disorders Association of America
8730 Georgia Avenue, Suite 600
Silver Spring, MD 20910
Tel: 1-240-485-1001
Online: http://www.adaa.org

National Institute of Mental Health
6001 Executive Boulevard, Room 8184, MSC 9663
Bethesda, MD 20892-9663
Tel: 1-301-443-4513
Online: http://www.nimh.nih.gov

Posttraumatic Stress Disorder Alliance
Tel: 1-877-507-7873
Online: http://www.ptsdalliance.org

The American Academy of Experts in Traumatic
   Stress
Administrative Offices
368 Veterans Memorial Highway
Commack, NY 11725
Tel: 1-631-543-2217
Online: http://www.aaets.org

The National Center for Post-Traumatic Stress
   Disorder
Online: http://www.ncptsd.org

CANADA

Canadian Traumatic Stress Network
Tel: 1-800-288-2876
Online: http://www.ctsn-rest.ca

ADDITIONAL RESOURCES

PREMATURITY
(Preterm Babies)

Prematurity/Preterm Babies refers to when a child is born more than three weeks early.

In assessing the size and weight of a child who was born prematurely, one must relate to the post-term age of the baby and not to his/her actual chronological age. Babies born prematurely grow at the intrauterine (prebirth) rate until the 35th week of the gestational period. From 35 to 40 weeks, they usually go through a growth spurt, reaching a low normal birth weight by the end of the normal gestation period. If they follow this sequence, they will usually have caught up to the norms in size by six to nine months after the time of birth. Some children who are born prematurely may not fully catch up until they are two or three years of age. In general, babies requiring more than one month in an intensive care nursery are more likely to have ongoing problems.

There has been an increase in recent years in the number of children who were preterm babies. This is due primarily to the increase in multiple births, as well as the fact that medical advances have resulted in the ability to keep infants alive who previously might not have survived.

Children who are born preterm may have physical and/or medical problems because of their small size and physical immaturity. This may lead to later problems in development.

ESSENTIAL INFORMATION	Alternative Considerations and Conditions	Recommendations
Though most babies who are born prematurely are perfectly normal, it is important to know those problems or deviations from the norm that are most frequently found. **1. Health** • Premature/preterm babies are often more susceptible to illness/infection during the first year of life. By the preschool years this is usually no longer true. **2. Vision** • Problems in this area frequently occur, especially in the area of eye muscle imbalance and nearsightedness. At times there is also some scarring in one or both eyes, causing partial blindness.	**Visual Impairment** **Fetal Alcohol Syndrome (FAS)/Fetal Alcohol Effect (FAE)/Maternal Substance Abuse**	• It is recommended that the teacher find out in the initial interview with the parents whether the child was full-term or preterm at birth. • If a child was born preterm, find out by how many weeks and whether there were any birth or postnatal complications. This may help staff in planning effectively for the child and in making more effective developmental assessments at a later time. • It is important to establish an ongoing dialogue with the parents, sharing observations and insights. If any problems are suspected, discuss these with the parents and seek a professional assessment and evaluation if necessary.

- Though previously retinopathy of prematurity (retrolental fibroplasia) causing blindness or severe vision problems often occurred in premature infants, with medical advances this now occurs much less frequently.

3. Hearing

- A hearing loss that is mainly in high frequency sounds is due to nerve deafness and is sometimes found as a result of preterm birth.

- Total deafness is rarely found.

4. Speech and Language

- Delays in receptive and/or expressive language frequently occur in low birth weight children

- Children who are born preterm will usually go through the normal sequences of babbling/prespeech–from single syllable sounds at three months, to inflection changes in tone, to more variety of consonant and vowel sounds by the ninth month

- By 18 months to two years of age, there may still be only a few recognizable words. Most preterm babies will catch up in speech and language during the preschool years.

5. Central Nervous System

- The most common problem found in this area is cerebral palsy–spastic form. This is often very mild.

Hearing Impairment

Speech and Language Problems
Note: One can usually rule out an intellectual disability if comprehension of language is age-appropriate.

Look for deviation from the normal pattern of muscle flexing.

- Specific programming should not be different from that of other children. Try to determine the developmental level and specific needs (for instance, in the language area), develop realistic expectations, and then design an appropriate program to meet the identified needs.

- Do stimulate verbal expression whenever possible, using props such as puppets and songs.

- If the child's rate of learning is below the norm in speech, receptive and/or expressive language, it should be recommended that the parents take the child for a hearing test and a speech and language assessment.

- Encourage participation in gross and fine motor activity.

- See recommendations under:
  –**Cerebral Palsy**
  –**Learning Disabilities/Sensory Integration Dysfunction**

- Depending on the degree of trauma at birth and how much illness occurred in the postnatal period, some children will have intellectual disabilities and/or specific learning disabilities. These may not be as evident in the preschool period and only become evident as the child enters the school system.

Cerebral Palsy

RESOURCES

LOCAL

Hospitals often offer follow-up support to families with preterm babies.

There are some hospitals and agencies that have special services for premature infants and their families. It is important to know which hospitals/ agencies in your immediate area can offer special support.

Public health agencies sometimes offer special support services.

UNITED STATES

American Association for Premature Infants
P.O. Box 46371
Cincinnati, OH 45246-0371
Tel: 1-513-956-4331
Online: http://www.aapi-online.org

Parents of Premature Babies Inc. (PREEMIE-L)
Online: http://www.preemie-1.org

Premature Baby Resource Web Sites
Online: http://www.prematurity.org/preemiepgs

March of Dimes
Online: http://www.modimes.com

ADDITIONAL RESOURCES

SICKLE CELL ANEMIA
(Sickle Cell Disease)

Sickle Cell Anemia is a chronic, inherited, genetic condition passed on by receiving a sickle cell gene from both parents. It is caused by a genetic change in hemoglobin, causing the red blood cells to take on the curved shape of a sickle. It can be identified prenatally by amniocentesis.

The sickle shaped red blood cells have a shorter life span than normal cells. This results in a lower red blood count, which in turn leads to anemia. Because the defective cells are less flexible and very sticky, it makes it difficult for them to deliver oxygen. This leads to pain and damage to body tissues and organs. Without the circulation of enough red blood cells, the body becomes deprived of oxygen. This leads to tiredness and fatigue.

Sickle cell anemia is most common in families of African American descent and is also found, though much less frequently, in families originating from the Mediterranean, Middle East, Asia, India, Caribbean, as well as Central and South America.

Sickle cell anemia is present at birth and is a lifelong disease. The definite symptoms can usually be recognized between the fourth to the sixth month. The amount of pain, as well as the specific complications, varies from one child to another. Comprehensive health care is extremely important. Treatment will usually relieve the symptoms of the condition and enable the individual to lead a relatively normal life, with generally good health, at least to middle age.

PHYSICAL CHARACTERISTICS	Important Questions to Ask	Recommendations
Physical signs and symptoms that may indicate the onset of a crisis: 1. Swollen hands and feet are often the first sign of sickle cell anemia in babies. This is often accompanied by pain (e.g., the child may scream when touched) and fever. 2. Periods of pain and swelling (sickling crises), predominantly in the chest, abdomen, and joints, are a major indication of sickle cell. These crises are caused when the sickled red blood cells block the blood flow through tiny blood vessels. The intensity of this pain may vary, and it may last for a few hours or as long as a few weeks. Sickling crises may be experienced very rarely in some	1. What are the symptoms this child exhibits on an ongoing basis? 2. Has he/she experienced a sickle cell crisis? If yes, what were the symptoms, how long did they last, what treatment was used, and so on? 3. Is the child on any ongoing medication or treatment? 4. Has the child received vaccinations for all childhood diseases? Be sure to get a list of which ones. 5. Has the child received yearly influenza shots? Has he/she been innoculated against pneumonia, and so on? ***Note:*** Vaccination against any and all diseases is extremely important for children	• Keep a daily log, recording any changes in behavior or physical health. • A day book should be kept in the center that is available for substitute teachers. This should include important information on this child, as well as other children with any type of special need(s). • If the child has been diagnosed as having sickle cell anemia prior to coming to the center, ask for a list of medical recommendations. • Find ways to include the child in all games and activities, even if his/her activity level is limited. This may mean developing special roles in certain games, e.g. scorekeeper or the person who is responsible for equipment, in active sports.

people, whereas in other people it may occur a number of times a year.

3. Jaundice from severe anemia results in the child experiencing one or more of the following:
   - Yellowed skin and/or eyes
   - Pale skin and lips
   - Feeling continually tired
   - Feeling very weak
   - Experiencing shortness of breath
   - Experiencing chest pain

Children with sickle cell anemia often

1. are vulnerable to **infections**. Sickle cells damage the spleen, the organ that filters germs out of the blood and makes antibodies to protect the person from infection. (**Note:** Physicians often put children with sickle cell anemia on continuous antibiotics to prevent life-threatening infectious conditions, such as pneumonia.) It is therefore important to watch for signs of infection, such as coughs, breathing trouble, crankiness, or a lack of appetite.

2. are prone to **dehydration**. Vomiting, diarrhea, and a lower quantity of urine are all signs that a child may be dehydrated.

3. are **stunted in growth**. Lack of red blood cells (the cells that provide oxygen and nutrients needed for the body to grow) can slow down growth in young

with sickle cell anemia in that they are more vulnerable to catching a disease and more likely to get a severe case of any disease they do catch.

6. Are there any special diet requirements and/or restrictions–especially with regard to fluid intake needs?

7. Are there any special precautions to take–especially with regard to preventing infections?

8. Does the child require more rest than other children his/her age? If yes, what is the symptom that will alert staff of the need for rest?

9. What is the child's physical activity level? Are there any limitations to what he/she can do?

10. Are there any restrictions with respect to going outside–especially in extremely warm, damp, or cold weather? If yes, get a written statement from the parents as to what these are.

11. What suggestions can the parents give to staff to help them to know what to do to make the child feel more comfortable if he/she is feeling sick or experiencing pain?

12. Are there specific signs to look for that might alert staff that the child is having a sickle cell crisis?

13. Who are the professionals involved in the child's health care? Is there a health caregiver that can support the center in

- Be prepared to have alternative program plans to switch to if he/she needs to take it easy for a while.

- Be accepting, treat the child as much like the other children as possible. Though the child with sickle cell anemia needs extra support in some areas, he/she needs limits as much as other children. The child may not be used to being told that he/she is expected to do something, or cannot do something he/she wishes to do, and staff may initially have to calmly, but firmly, explain why this limit is necessary. It is important *not* to be oversolicitous and/or overprotective of the child.

- Try to support the child and help him/her to deal with any social and/or emotional problems resulting from the disease.

- If the child has been hospitalized, or is about to be, develop some special learning centers and/or pretend play areas around this experience–for example, a medical center; or a community people project, including doctors, nurses, ambulance workers, and so on.

- Keep a communication book (to be shared between the home and the center) in which important information can be recorded, giving date, time, place, circumstances, and signature of staff involved; activities in which the child excelled, or in which he/she experienced some difficulties; new friendships, and so on.

children and delay puberty in older children.

4. experience **vision problems**. Damage to the retina (retinopathy) can be caused by blocking of the tiny blood vessels that lead to the eyes.

Additional complications from sickle cell anemia include the possibility of

- stroke.
- lung infections and lung damage.
- kidney, liver, and/or spleen complications.
- blindness caused by retina damage.
- joint problems.
- leg ulcers or open sores.

understanding the disease and developing an enriched program for the child?

14. Has the child had to undergo any extreme treatment—such as blood transfusions, bone marrow transplant, surgery, and so on? If yes, when, how long was the hospitalization, how did the child react, and so on?

15. When should staff call the parents and/or the child's physician? What hospital should be contacted/used if an emergency should arise?

- *Note:* It is a good idea to share staff observations with the parents, add parents comments and suggestions, and have them initial and date the final copy that will go into the child's file.

- Be sure to have an "Emergency System" posted in case a substitute staff or parent-helper should be present.

- Families of other children in the center need to be made aware of how important it is to let the center know if their child contracts an infection.

- A Medic Alert bracelet is recommended.

- Try to investigate the availability of a parent support group for the child's family.

RESOURCES

LOCAL

Hospitals

Local chapters of organizations serving children with sickle cell, sickle cell anemia, or sickle cell disease

UNITED STATES

American Sickle Cell Anemia Association
10300 Carnegie Avenue
Cleveland, OH 44106
Tel: 1-216-229-8600
Online: http://www.ascaa.org

Sickle Cell Disease Association of America Inc.
200 Corporate Pointe, Suite 495
Culver City, CA 90230-8727
Tel: 1-800-421-8453
Online: http://sicklecelldisease.org

CANADA

The Sickle Cell Association of Ontario
3199 Bathurst Street, Suite 202
Toronto, Ontario M6A 2B2
Tel: 1-416-789-2855
Online: http://sicklecellontario.com

Sickle Cell Information Center
Grady Memorial Hospital
P.O. Box 109
80 Jessie Hill Jr. Drive SE
Atlanta, GA 30303
Tel: 1-404-616-3572
Online: http://www.scinfo.org

ADDITIONAL RESOURCES

SPEECH AND LANGUAGE PROBLEMS

Speech impairments are problems encountered in the oral production of language.

Language problems involve a lack of understanding (receptive) and/or using language (expressive) and written communication.

Children may encounter some of the following problems at any time in the development of their speech and/or language.

Note: Most children are able to communicate verbally before three years of age. By seven or eight years of age, a child should be able to articulate all sounds.

SPEECH

PHYSICAL AND BEHAVIORAL CHARACTERISTICS	Alternative Considerations and Conditions	Recommendations

The child with speech problems may
 	
1. have open mouth position, often breathing through the mouth.
 	
2. have excessive drooling, resulting from weakness of the jaw, tongue, and/or lips.
 	
3. have poor eating habits–for example, messy, limited swallowing and chewing.
 	
4. become easily frustrated, stamping feet and blinking eyes.
 	
5. have frequent upper respiratory and ear infections; frequent absenteeism.
 	
6. lack eye contact.
 	
7. have poor oral motor coordination.
 	
8. not have babbled as an infant.
 	
Articulation/Speech Sounds
 	
The child's symptoms may include
 	
1. distortions of standard sounds.
	Enlarged tonsils
	Nodules
	Allergies
	
	Intellectual Disabilities
	Cerebral Palsy
	Cleft Lip/Palate
	Cultural Influences/English as a Second Language/English with a Dialect
	Developmental and/or maturational lags
	Tension (Is pressure being placed on the child?)
	
	Autism Spectrum Disorder
	
	Cultural Influences/English as a Second Language/English with a Dialect
		• Inform parents if there are any concerns.
		
		• Model correct pronunciation, incorporating in the next sentence the word that the child has mispronounced, but *not* calling the child's attention to it.
		
		• Observe and record situations when and where tension occurs and in what way it does/does not impact on the child's speech/language.
		
		• Encourage good chewing during mealtimes.
		
		• Try to involve the child in activities that involve speaking, but do not single him/her out in any way.
		  –house-corner dramatic play
		  –singing and chanting games
		  –puppet play
		
		• A physical checkup is recommended.
		
		• A hearing test is recommended.

2. substitutions of one sound for another.

3. omission of sounds that should be present.

4. irrelevant sounds.

Voice Sounds

The child's voice may be unusual due to

1. quality (hoarse, nasal, breathy, and/or husky).

2. pitch (monotone, too high, or too low).

3. intensity (volume) (too loud or too soft).

Fluency (rhythm)

The child may exhibit

1. hesitations.

2. repetitions.

3. prolongations.

4. blockages when attempting to speak, such as stuttering (dysfluency), stammering.

LANGUAGE

PHYSICAL AND BEHAVIORAL CHARACTERISTICS

The child with language problems may

1. have or have had frequent ear infections.

2. be hyperactive or hypoactive.

3. have poor motor coordination.

Hearing Impairment

Cleft Lip/Palate
Cerebral Palsy
Developmental delay

Lack of experience (has not heard correct pronunciation)

Enlarged tonsils/adenoids
Missing teeth

Nodules

Cleft Lip/Palate

Hearing Impairment

Poor speech models
Developmental process in which the child may think faster than he/she can form words (this is of no consequence and usually passes)
Behavioral/Social/Emotional Problems

Alternative Considerations and Conditions

Hearing Impairment

Attention Deficit/Hyperactive Disorder

Motor Problems

- A speech assessment is recommended.

- Remember that at all times the teacher is acting as a role model for the child.

- Model correct pronunciation.

- Record (using tape recorder, video recorder, or in written format) a sample of the child's speech patterns.

- *Do not* interrupt the child.

- *Do not* rush the child.

- *Do not* pressure or demand that the child talk.

- Look at the child while he/she is talking.

- Model smooth speech.

- Observe and record other developmental skills and/or difficulties.

- Carry out an informal developmental assessment.

- Obtain the child's attention before speaking to him/her.

- Use simple, uncomplicated language.

- Name and label objects.

- Develop games in which the child learns to recognize animal and environmental sounds.

- Provide activities for listening, such as giving instructions and having the child follow them.

- Model language, cuing the child nonverbally.

4. lack body/eye contact.

5. repeat certain verbal responses over and over.

6. become easily frustrated or distracted.

7. have a poor attention span.

8. have poor learning how-to-learn skills.

9. perform better on nonverbal tasks than verbal tasks.

10. have delayed preacademic and academic skills.

Receptive Language (Comprehension).
The child has difficulty understanding the spoken word.

The child may

1. have a history of delayed language development.

2. have poor listening skills.

3. cover his/her ears; lack or avoid eye contact; and/or turn away.

4. understand only a few words or phrases.

5. find it difficult to follow simple commands.

6. not carry out verbal instructions unless accompanied by gestures.

7. not attend to class discussions, stories, or group time (tunes out).

8. have a short attention span.

9. frequently repeat what the teacher has said.

Autism Spectrum Disorder

Attention Deficit/Hyperactive Disorder

Learning Disabilities

Attention Deficit/Hyperactive Disorder

Cultural Influences/English as a Language/English with a Dialect

Developmental delay
Prematurity (Preterm)

Hearing Impairment
Ear infection
Overly sensitive hearing
Fear in new situations
Cultural Influences/English as a Second Language/English with a Dialect

Intellectual Disabilities
Deprived home environment

First experience in a structured setting
Autism Spectrum Disorder

- Encourage indoor and outdoor dramatic play.

- Involve the child in short, satisfying experiences. Remember that his/her attention span for listening is likely to be shorter than that of other children of his/her age.

- Make frequent eye contact with the child.

- Praise the child for correct responses.

- Talk about what the child is doing.

- Give information clearly.

- Read simple stories, stressing sequencing.

- Describe events in stories, using visual clues.

- Use songs and tapes to facilitate listening skills.

- Provide repetition to help the child remember and learn new words.

- Provide plenty of visual and tactile experiences; bring in concrete objects when introducing a new idea.

- Give the child experiential learning such as cooking activities; neighborhood walks; trips to farms, stores, fire station, post office, bakery, and so on.

- Plan themes and follow up with opportunities for sequential learning, using experiential (physically acting out) activities, pictures, and trips to clarify concepts.

- Use repetition and a variety of media to ensure that the concept is correctly comprehended.

10. ask for frequent repetitions of instructions.

11. have inappropriate facial expressions or appear confused when listening.

12. not retain new words taught.

13. appear to have good verbal skills but quality of content is limited.

14. find it difficult to remember the sequence of tasks in pictures used to tell a familiar story.

15. respond to only part of information, possibly an unimportant detail.

16. not have a sense of humor, not be able to find absurdities in pictures, and so on.

17. have difficulty classifying objects in pictures.

18. have difficulty choosing the correct answer to a question if not given physical or visual cues.

19. have difficulty remembering important personal information, such as address and phone number.

20. have problems with reading, especially use of phonetic skills.

21. have difficulty in keeping track of where he/she is when doing seatwork or reading.

22. not understand what he/she has read.

23. have problems with spelling.

Attention Deficit /Hyperactive Disorder
Learning Disabilities
Hearing Impairment
Behavioral/Social/Emotional Problems

Cultural Influences/English as a Second Language/English with a Dialect

Attention Deficit/Hyperactive Disorder

Learning Disabilities

Visual Impairment
Hearing Impairment

Spatial disorientation

- Provide matching games (lotto-type).

- Try to involve parents, encouraging them to carry out parallel types of activities at home. The center should use a communication book, which gives brief feedback on ideas to talk about, activities to encourage at home, and notes on experiences the child has had in school.

- Record a sample of the child's language patterns, for the purpose of gathering clues as to how he/she comprehends.

- Make sure that staff do not draw attention to the child's difficulty.

- Model correct language, incorporating the child's idea when responding to the child.

- Expand on the child's utterances by additional comments.

- Allow the child to answer questions at his/her level, praising any attempt he/she makes.

- Encourage communication by choosing activities that facilitate language, such as games in which the child has to express his/her needs.

- Help the child obtain the correct response by providing visual clues and modeling the correct response, if necessary.

- Praise the child for correct responses.

- Give the child as much time as needed to express him-/herself.

Expressive Language (Oral and Written)
The child has difficulty expressing his/her ideas.

The child may

1. not have babbled as an infant.

2. not use any gestures or sounds to communicate.

3. use many nonverbal gestures and sounds to communicate.

4. have a history of delayed language.

5. have language that is immature; may use only simple word combinations, such as nouns and verbs.

6. have limited vocabulary.

7. have improper use of words and word order.

8. be unable to relate events with ideas (ideas are jumbled, not in logical sequence, therefore the child worries about changes in routines or what is happening next).

9. express ideas but in a disorganized fashion.

10. respond inappropriately to questions or situations.

11. find it difficult to retrieve and recall words he/she knows.

12. find it difficult to describe items or situations without visual clues.

13. have frequent grammatical errors.

Developmental delay
Deprived home environment

Poor speech models at home

First experience in a structured setting and child is scared/withdrawn.

Cultural Influences/English as a Second Language/English with a Dialect

Learning Disabilities

Attention Deficit/Hyperactive Disorder

Hearing Impairment

Environmental

- If a child has mispronunciations, or poor word order, *do not* make the child repeat it correctly, but model the correct pronunciation/word order in the next sentence.

- Start with simple language constructions, such as nouns and verbs, then work up to more complex ones, such as simple phrases and simple sentences.

- Provide multiple verbal and visual choices for a child who may have problems recalling a desired word.

- Plan experiential activities like trips that can be followed up with recall through dramatic play, writing/dictating stories, conversation, pictures, and so on.

- Develop a pictorial chart of attributes to augment the child's descriptive vocabulary, clarifying concepts through pictures that demonstrate quantity, quality, size, shape, position in space, and/or color.

- Provide many opportunities for group interactions through singing, finger plays/body movement games, nursery rhymes, and stories.

- Concepts such as position in space and quantity can also be taught through music and body movement.

- Involve the child in small group play and interactions as often as possible.

- Try to maintain eye contact as much as possible (in order to be sure the child is aware of what is going on in the class).

14. use incomplete sentences (nouns, pronouns, or verbs may be missing).

15. communicate well on topics of his/her choice, but avoid teacher-chosen topics.

16. have immediate (repeating words just heard) or delayed echolalia (repeating words heard in the past).

17. be able to express ideas and use words effectively, but is selective as to where or to whom he/she will talk.

18. have previously talked and then stopped talking.

19. not spontaneously contribute ideas or initiate conversation unless coaxed.

20. find it difficult to sequence numbers or letters in the alphabet.

21. have poor printing skills.

22. have difficulty with reading (sounding out words).

23. have more difficulty than most children with early written communication.

24. exhibit delayed social behavior; poor peer interaction.

Autism Spectrum Disorder

Cultural Influences/English as a Second Language/English with a Dialect

**Behavioral/Social/Emotional Problems
Elective/Selective Mutism
Autism Spectrum Disorder**

Learning Disabilities

Motor Problems

Cultural Influences/English as a Second Language/English with a Dialect
No English written or spoken in the home

Abuse/Neglect
Little experience with peers

- Do not push the child to read. Language development is a prerequisite for reading.

Remember: Opportunities for success are extremely important.

Note: A speech and language assessment is recommended.

See **Augmentative Communication Systems** under **Cerebral Palsy.**

RESOURCES

LOCAL

Many hospitals have speech and language clinics that will provide individual treatment.

UNITED STATES

American Speech-Language-Hearing Association
10801 Rockville Pike
Rockville, MD 20852
Tel: 1-800-638-8255
Online: http://www.asha.org

CANADA

Canadian Association of Speech-Language Pathologists and Audiologists (CASLPA)
401-200 Elgin Street
Ottawa, Ontario K2P 1L5
Tel: 1-800-259-8519
Online: http://www.caslpa.ca

Check for local speech clinics and agencies that provide support in language and speech development—hearing, learning disabilities, and so on.

Boards of Education (Special Education).

Hearing Speech Deafness Center
1620 18th Avenue
Seattle, WA 98122
Tel: 1-206-323-5770
Online: http://www.hsdc.org

National Information Center for Children and
    Youth with Disabilities
P.O. Box 1492
Washington, DC 20013-1492
Tel: 1-800-695-0285
Online: http://www.nichcy.org

National Institute on Deafness and Other
    Communication Disorders
National Institutes of Health
31 Center Drive, MSC 2320
Bethesda, MD 20892-2320
Online: http://www.nidcd.nih.gov

Speech-Language Pathology Web Sites
Online: http. //speech-language pathologist.org

Ontario Association for Families of Children with
    Communication Disorders (OAFCCD)
13 Segal Drive
Tillsonburg, Ontario N4G 4P4
Tel: 1-519-842-9506
Online: http://www.oaffccd.com

The Hanen Centre
1075 Bay Street Suite 515
Toronto, Ontario M5S 2B1
Tel: 1-416-921-1073
Online: http://www.hanen.org

Toronto Children's Centre
10 Buchan Court
Toronto, Ontario M2J 1V2
Tel: 1-416-491-7771
Online: http://www.speechfoundation.org

ADDITIONAL RESOURCES

SPINA BIFIDA
(Neural Tube Defects [NTD])

Spina Bifida (neural tube defects [NTD]) is caused by prenatal abnormalities of the brain and/or spinal cord and their protective coverings, resulting in an opening in the vertebral column, often involving the central nervous system. This condition can vary a great deal in degree of severity. In some children, it may merely involve a weakness in one part of the spine; whereas in other cases, there may be a complete exposure of part of the spinal cord. Symptoms of the more severe form may include:

1. loss of sensation from the spina bifida protrusion to all areas of the body below it.
2. little or no bladder or bowel control.
3. hydrocephalus, which may be corrected through the implantation of shunts.
4. brittle bones in areas in which there is poor circulation due to lack of sensation and physical movement.
5. loss of muscle control below spine lesion.

In recent years, all women who are planning to become pregnant are advised to take folic acid, which has been found to reduce the likelihood of neural tube defects.

Note: **The child with spina bifida (neural tube defects) will come to the center prediagnosed.**

IMPORTANT QUESTIONS TO ASK	Essential Information	Recommendations
1. What is the extent of the child's mobility? Is the child in a walker, wheelchair, caliphers, braces, or other apparatus? 2. What is the extent of his/her mobility? 3. What is the extent of his/her sensation? 4. What parts of his/her body are affected—legs, hips, and so on? 5. What are his/her recognized limitations? 6. Is the child toilet trained? What is the toileting routine and procedure? Must the teacher know how to replace a catheter? What help does the child need with bowel movements?	Because there are certain environmental and physical needs, it is important to think about whether the center is equipped to provide an effective program for the child. Does the center have stairs, narrow hallways, washrooms that are inaccessible, or is the center relatively easy to enter and circulate in it? Are there enough staff available to • support the level of individual physical needs of the child? • provide as many activities and opportunities as possible to help the child feel a sense of belonging, acceptance and achievement?	*Note:* The primary goal should be to enable the child to participate as fully as possible in the ongoing program and develop positive social/emotional interactions with his/her peer group. • Encourage special skills such as art, painting, music, and clay. • See program suggestions listed under Recommendations for **Cerebral Palsy** and **Motor Problems**.

7. Are there any special needs with regard to blood circulation; for example, does the child need to be moved frequently? Is there any history of limb breakage due to brittleness of bones? Is there a history of hip dislocation?

8. If the child has hydrocephalus, does he/she have shunts implanted? Are there any side effects to note? If there is clogging of the shunts, what physical sign/complaint may alert the teacher to this problem? What procedure should be followed?

9. Who is the physician attending to the child?

10. What agency is presently working with the child? Who is the person to contact for support in understanding therapeutic objectives? Will they provide ongoing consultation to the center?

11. What expectations do the parents have of the center/staff?

Other conditions sometimes associated with children who have spina bifida that should be checked out:

- Is there any history of a latex allergy (this may occur if the child has had many surgeries/casts)?

- Any evidence of tendinitis?

- Is there a tendency towards obesity?

- Are there any skin problems?

- Is there any history of gastrointestinal problems?

- enable the child to become an integral part of the group?

Can emergency procedures be adapted to include the needs of the child in a fire or accident?

It is important that there is a clear understanding between the center and the child's parents and physician that regular staff are not physiotherapists; that they will support the therapeutic program suggestions (special positions, regular moving of position, specific types of physical action) as much as possible; however, it must be questioned as to whether these will adequately meet the needs of the child.

Alternative Considerations and Conditions

Allergies (not related to the spina bifida)

HYDROCEPHALUS

Many of the children with the more severe form of Spina Bifida have Hydrocephalus.

Hydrocephalus is a condition in which there is an excessive buildup of spinal fluid on the brain. If this fluid is left to accumulate, the child's head will become progressively larger and brain damage will occur. To avoid the buildup of fluid, pliable plastic shunts are surgically inserted beneath the skin to drain off the excessive fluid from the brain into the body cavities.

At times, a shunt may malfunction. Typical symptoms of shunt malfunction are

- vomiting.
- lethargy.
- irritability.
- seizures.
- headaches.
- redness or swelling in the neck, head, or around the shunts.
- crossing of eyes/drooping eyelids.
- in infants, the fontanel (soft spot on head) bulges.

Note: If it is suspected that a shunt is malfunctioning, the child's parents and physician should be consulted at once. The child should be taken to a hospital if no one can be reached.

RESOURCES

LOCAL

Spinal cord and spina bifida associations and organizations

Special provisions within the educational system

Hospitals, clinics, and local agencies providing services for physically handicapped person

UNITED STATES

Spina Bifida Association of America
4590 MacArthur Boulevard NW, Suite 250
Washington, DC 20007-4226
Tel: 1-800-621-3141
Online: http://www.sbaa.org

The Hydrocephalus Foundation Inc. (HyFI)
910 Rear Broadway, Rt. 1
Saugus, MA 01906
Tel: 1-718-942-1161
Online: http://www.hydrocephalus.org

CANADA

Spina Bifida and Hydrocephalus Association of Canada
167 Lombard Avenue, Suite 977
Winnipeg, Manitoba R3B OV3
Tel: 1-800-565-9488
Online: http://www.sbhac.ca

ADDITIONAL RESOURCES

TOURETTE SYNDROME (TS) and BEHAVIORAL TICS

Tics are involuntary, repeated contractions of one or more muscles. Though they may involve squinting or grimacing, they are painless.

Most tics last for relatively short periods of time, often during periods of high stress, and then pass, usually lasting less than a year. There is one chronic condition involving tics: Tourette Syndrome.

Tourette Syndrome is a neurological disorder in which the individual experiences involuntary, multiple tics (muscular jerking), affecting the head, arms, legs, and at times vocalization.

Symptoms usually occur many times a day, nearly every day. Tourette Syndrome is usually first recognized between 5 and 10 years of age, and is found more frequently in males.

The majority of children with Tourette Syndrome have had other family members with tic disorders.

Treatment: Most people with behavioral tics are not significantly disabled. When symptoms interfere with functioning, there is medication that can be taken to help the individual control his/her symptoms. Many people with Tourette Syndrome can learn to control (hold in) their tic behavior for a period of time, but usually need to release the inhibited behaviors after the period of control.

PHYSICAL CHARACTERISTICS	Alternative Considerations and Conditions	Recommendations
Involuntary motor movements and symptoms which are common in Tourette Syndrome include: • head jerking. • facial grimacing. • repetitive eye blinking and/or squinting. • repetitive nose movement/twitching. • clicking of tongue. • repetitive movements of the shoulders and arms. • body scratching. • repetitive leg jerking. • repetitive foot tapping. • repetitive vocal sounds, including meaningless noises, grunts, barks, hoots, hisses, squeaks, gurgles, snorts, and so on. • echoing sounds or phrases over and over again.	Nervous twitches and tics (non-Tourette) Eye conditions and sensitivities Nervous habits **Autism Spectrum Disorder** **Oppositional Defiant Disorder Learning Disabilities**	• If the child with Tourette Syndrome is being teased by other children, it is important to talk to the other children when the child is not in the room. Let the children know that this is not intentional behavior and that their friend cannot control his/her actions. One can compare it to something the other children have experienced, such as hiccuping. • Try to ignore the tic behavior as much as possible. If there are disruptive noises, this may at times be difficult. Sometimes one can distract the child or get him/her involved in an activity and the noises may stop. • Be aware that periods of excitement (doing a play or concert, going on a trip), are likely to increase the tic behavior.

Many children with Tourette Syndrome also experience the following associated behavior problems:

- Attention deficits
- Obsessive compulsive disorder (more common in girls)
- Conduct disorders
- Oppositional defiant disorder
- Learning disabilities
- Sleep problems

Social and emotional problems may develop if the child has not had opportunities for positive peer relationships and/or has parents who have been over-protective or unable to know how to handle his/her behavior.

Attention Deficit/Hyperactive Disorder

- It is important to work with a specialist who can help teachers to know what goals are realistic for this child. The symptoms and related behaviors in Tourette Syndrome have a broad range from minimal to very severe and pervasive.

Note: The tic behaviors are likely to decrease in severity and frequency, as the child becomes more comfortable in his/her environment.

IMPORTANT QUESTIONS TO ASK

1. It is important to find out in what ways the Tourette Syndrome impacts on the behavior of the child. What specific behavioral tics are likely to be seen?

2. How frequently does the child manifest these behaviors?

3. Are there specific types of situations that seem to trigger tics or other related behaviors?

4. Is there a specific time of day in which the behavior seems to be more evident?

5. Many children with Tourette Syndrome experience more evident tic behavior around holidays and times when major

Essential Information

There is no known prevention or cure for Tourette Syndrome.

If you suspect that a child in the center has undiagnosed Tourette Syndrome, it is important to recommend that the parents have the child examined by a qualified physician.

Children with minor symptoms are often not treated because the medications currently used can have side effects that may result in symptoms worse than the Tourette. There are, however, some medications that have been effective in some children who have Tourette Syndrome with debilitating behaviors.

changes are likely to occur—for example, beginning of school year, prior to a vacation time, end of school year, and so on. Have the parents noticed a similar pattern of behavior in their child?

Tourette Syndrome in children may become more intense in adolescence and then gradually diminish during adulthood.

If the child with Tourette Syndrome has been controlling a tic behavior, he/she may need time and a place after the period of control, for releasing the tension and tic behavior.

People with Tourette Syndrome may be able to learn to control some of the tic motions or sounds for a short period of time; however, when they can no longer control them, the tics may be more intense than usual when they occur.

RESOURCES

LOCAL

Hospital clinics and programs specializing in Tourette Syndrome are available in some areas.

Local organizations and associations can offer family support.

UNITED STATES

National Tourette Syndrome Association Inc.
42-40 Bell Boulevard
Bayside, NY 11361
Tel: 1-718-224-2999
Online: http://www.tsa-usa.org

CANADA

Tourette Syndrome Foundation of Canada
194 Jarvis Street, Suite 206
Toronto, Ontario M5B 2B7
Tel: 1-800-361-3120
Online: http://www.tourette.ca

ADDITIONAL RESOURCES

TRAUMATIC BRAIN INJURY (TBI)
(Brain Trauma)

Traumatic Brain Injury (TBI) is caused by a sudden physical force or assault to the head that causes damage to the brain. One or more areas of the brain may be affected. Injuries may range from a mild concussion to coma or even death. Treatment usually involves surgery to control bleeding in and around the brain.

Head injuries sustained by young children that may lead to Traumatic Brain Injury include:
- falls from heights.
- abuse—baby shaking, dropping of the child, and so on.
- blows to the head.
- sports accidents.
- car/bike accidents.

More serious Traumatic Brain Injury may result in:
- physical damage (tearing of brain fibers)
- swelling, resulting in pressure on the brain
- bleeding or blood clotting within the brain.

PHYSICAL AND EMOTIONAL BEHAVIORS	Essential Information	Recommendations

Some symptoms that children with Traumatic Brain Injury may experience include:
• fractured skull.
• serious bleeding from head and/or face.
• loss of consciousness (no matter how brief).
• lack of pulse.
• confusion or drowsiness.
• blood or clear fluid leaking from the nose or ears.
 	
Symptoms (sometimes delayed) that may occur and should not be ignored include:
• severe headaches.
• loss of memory and confusion.
	Note: **If a child should experience injury in the school/child care program,** *immediately:*
	  1. follow First Aid procedures.
	  2. call for an ambulance.
	  3. call parents or designated person.
	
	Important Questions to Ask
	
	If the injury occurred prior to admittance to the center:
	  1. What was the nature of the extreme traumatic situation that occurred?
		• If an injury occurs at the center, it is important to make the child comfortable, while at the same time trying to keep him/her conscious while waiting for help. Ice should be applied to bumps to curtail swelling. Measures should be taken to stop bleeding.
		
		• Other children who have witnessed the accident need to be reassured and given an opportunity to express any concerns.

- vomiting.
- dizziness, loss of balance.
- numbness and/or partial paralysis.
- shock (rapid pulse, gray-blue skin coloring, sweaty and/or clammy skin).
- anxiety.
- blurry or double vision.

Later symptoms may include:
- lowered mental capacity.
- post-traumatic stress disorder.

Most frequent physical problems encountered, include:
- speech problems.
- vision problems.
- hearing problems.
- fine motor problems.
- problems in short and long term memory.
- shortened attention span.

2. When did the incident occur?

3. Have the parents noted any behavior changes? If yes, when did the changes begin to occur and what was the nature of the changes?

4. Have the parents noted any new fears that the child is experiencing?

5. Have the parents noticed any changes in the child's play and/or drawings? Does the child seem to be replaying the incident in his/her play and/or artwork?

6. Is the child showing signs of fear around activities similar to the one in which the injury occurred? If yes, describe what has been noted.

7. Is the child on any medication?

- **Children who have experienced a Traumatic Brain Injury** may need to talk about what happened to them. It is important to listen and help the child to understand. Whenever possible, supportive responses should be given by the teacher.

- The child may need to "play out" the trauma he/she experienced through:
  –dramatic play.

  –sensory materials such as paint or clay.

  –telling a story, which a teacher can record for him/her.

RESOURCES

LOCAL

Local hospitals and public health personnel may have written materials which can be kept on hand at the center.

UNITED STATES

Brain Trauma Foundation
523 East 72nd Street, 8th Floor
New York, NY 10021
Tel: 212-772-0608
Online: http://www.braintrauma.org

Brain Injury Association
105 North Alfred Street
Alexandria, VA 22314
Tel: 703-236-6000
Online: http://www.biausa.org

CANADA

Canadian Brain Injury Coalition
29 Pearce Avenue
Winnipeg, Manitoba R2V 2K3
Tel: 204-334-0471
Online: http://www.cbic.ca

ADDITIONAL RESOURCES

VISUAL IMPAIRMENT

Visual Impairment refers to a condition in which visual acuity is not sufficient for the child to participate with ease in everyday activities. It refers to people who have never had any visual functioning, as well as those who became gradually or suddenly partially or totally blind. It is important to be aware of the specific circumstances of the child with a visual impairment in order to develop appropriate goals and program plans to meet his/her physical, social, emotional, and learning needs.

PHYSICAL CHARACTERISTICS	Alternative Considerations and Conditions	Recommendations

The child's eyes may
 	
1. be inflamed or watery.
 	
2. have reoccurring styes or infections.
 	
3. be red-rimmed, encrusted, and/or have swollen eyelids.
 	
4. have pupils of different size.
 	
5. have drooping eyelids.
 	
6. be sensitive to light.
 	
7. see well one day and not the next.
 	
8. be crossed, resulting in an abnormal alignment of the gaze of one or both of the eyes.
 	
9. be semiclosed or squinted.
 	
10. have muscular problems in which one eye may appear to be focusing in an opposite direction from the other (strabismus).
	Eye infections
	
	Allergies
		• Record observations of the child's reaction to different environments, at different times of the day, and in response to different foods (in case of allergic reaction). Keep a record of when the child
		
		  –holds an object or picture very close.
		
		  –bends over a task with his/her head extremely close to the picture, blocks, toys, and books.
		
		  –squints when looking at something in the distance.
		
		  –bends his/her head, and appears to be using one eye to see something.
		
		  –covers one eye when looking at an object, and so on.
		
		• Check the child's records and inform the child's parents or physician if there is a problem that is interfering with the child's motor development and/or learning.
		
		• Recommend that the child have a physical and specifically an eye checkup (visual acuity and visual perception).
		
		• Present objects at different visual angles; show moving as well as stationary objects.

BEHAVIORAL CHARACTERISTICS

The child may

1. rub his/her eyes excessively, shut or cover one eye, blink or squint more than usual.

2. tilt or thrust his/her head forward; have a distorted facial expression.

3. have sore or burning eyes, blurred or double vision.

4. complain of dizziness, headaches, nausea, or being unable to see.

5. stumble and trip over small objects.

6. be delayed in cognitive, fine or gross motor, language and/or social emotional development.

7. avoid visual activities such as books, drawing, small peg boards, and puzzles.

8. hold objects close to, or far away from eyes; lean over objects to observe more closely; squint or make errors if distant vision is required (objects pointed out on a trip, outdoor games, objects requested from across the room).

9. exhibit inattentive behavior, especially when visual attention is required.

10. have trouble finding an object that is part of a picture.

11. have trouble with beginning reading and/or math.

Hearing Impairment

Behavioral/Social/Emotional Problems

Viral infection

Motor Problems
Cerebral Palsy

Note: Children who have had a recent growth spurt often go through a period of poor coordination. Poorly fitting shoes may also make the child seem uncoordinated.

Hearing Impairment
Behavioral/Social/Emotional Problems

Intellectual Disabilities

- Accompany presentations, directions, and so on with as many verbal descriptions as possible.

- Maintain good lighting.

- Note whether the child becomes tense, passive, or avoids certain situations.

- Give the child more attention at times when he/she is not involved in attention-getting behaviors, noting whether there are any changes in behavior that take place.

12. have trouble distinguishing between colors–for example, red and green, blue and yellow. (*Note:* Color blindness is present at birth and occurs mainly in boys).

Note: The child may have peripheral vision that is stronger than his/her overall visual ability. Check for lack of eye contact, tilting of head, and other body posturing that might indicate this problem.

Autism Spectrum Disorder

RESOURCES

LOCAL

Hospital eye clinics

Board of education services, special classes, books

Local chapters of organizations serving the visually impaired

UNITED STATES

American Foundation for the Blind
11 Penn Plaza, Suite 300
New York, NY 10001
Tel: 1-800-392-3305
Online: http://www.afb.org

American Optometric Association
243 North Lindbergh Boulevard
St. Louis, MO 63141
Tel: 1-314-991-4100
Online: http://www.aoanet.org

Blind Babies Foundation
5016 Mission Street
San Francisco, CA 94112
Tel: 1-415-586-6140
Online: http://www.blindbabies.org

Blind Childrens Center
4120 Marathon Street
Los Angelos, CA 90029
Tel: 1-323-664-2153
Online: http://www.blindcntr.org

CANADA

Canadian Association of Optometrists
234 Argyle Avenue
Ottawa, Ontario K2P 1B9
Tel: 1-613-235-7924
Online: http://www.opto.ca

Canadian National Institute for the Blind
National Office
1929 Bayview Avenue
Toronto, Ontario M4G 3E8
Tel: 1-416-486-2500
Online: http://www.cnib.ca

Canadian Opthalmological Society
1525 Carling Avenue, Suite 610
Ottawa, Ontario K1Z 8R9
Tel: 1-800-267-5763
Online: http://www.eyesite.ca

Vision Institute of Canada
16 York Mills Road Suite 110
Toronto, Ontario M2P 2E5
Tel: 1-416-224-2273
Online: http://www.visioninstitute.optometry.net

International Eye Foundation
10801 Connecticut Avenue
Kensington, MD 20895
Tel: 1-240-290-0263 or 1-240-290-0264
Online: http://www.iefusa.org

National Eye Institute
2020 Vision Place
Bethesda, MD 20892-3655
Tel: 1-301-496-5248
Online: http://www.nei.nih.gov

ADDITIONAL RESOURCES

DEVELOPMENTAL SEQUENCES FOR OBSERVING AND FORMULATING INDIVIDUALIZED PROGRAM PLANS

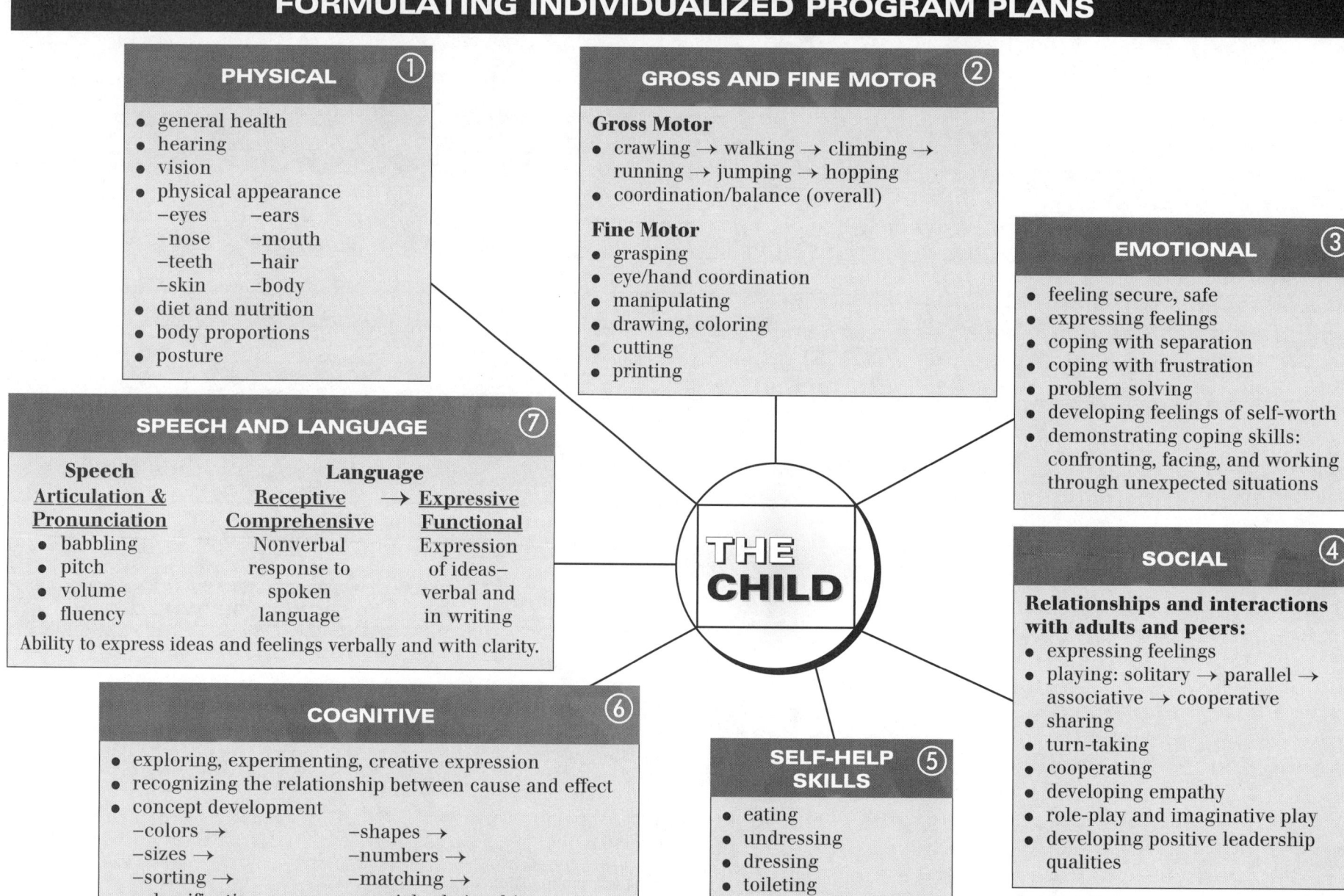

PHYSICAL ①

- general health
- hearing
- vision
- physical appearance
  - –eyes   –ears
  - –nose   –mouth
  - –teeth   –hair
  - –skin   –body
- diet and nutrition
- body proportions
- posture

GROSS AND FINE MOTOR ②

Gross Motor
- crawling → walking → climbing → running → jumping → hopping
- coordination/balance (overall)

Fine Motor
- grasping
- eye/hand coordination
- manipulating
- drawing, coloring
- cutting
- printing

EMOTIONAL ③

- feeling secure, safe
- expressing feelings
- coping with separation
- coping with frustration
- problem solving
- developing feelings of self-worth
- demonstrating coping skills: confronting, facing, and working through unexpected situations

SPEECH AND LANGUAGE ⑦

Speech	**Language**	
Articulation & Pronunciation	**Receptive Comprehensive**	→ **Expressive Functional**
• babbling	Nonverbal	Expression
• pitch	response to	of ideas–
• volume	spoken	verbal and
• fluency	language	in writing

Ability to express ideas and feelings verbally and with clarity.

THE CHILD

SOCIAL ④

Relationships and interactions with adults and peers:
- expressing feelings
- playing: solitary → parallel → associative → cooperative
- sharing
- turn-taking
- cooperating
- developing empathy
- role-play and imaginative play
- developing positive leadership qualities

COGNITIVE ⑥

- exploring, experimenting, creative expression
- recognizing the relationship between cause and effect
- concept development
  - –colors →   –shapes →
  - –sizes →   –numbers →
  - –sorting →   –matching →
  - –classification →   –spatial relationships →
  - –symbolic representation (letters and numerals) →
- problem solving

SELF-HELP SKILLS ⑤

- eating
- undressing
- dressing
- toileting
- personal grooming

INDEX